G000278586

Once Upon
an
EGG

by
Roy Porter

Grosvenor House
Publishing Limited

This book is published by
Grosvenor House Publishing Ltd
28-30 High Street, Guildford, Surrey, GU1 3EL.
www.grosvenorhousepublishing.co.uk

A CIP record for this book
is available from the British Library

ISBN **978-1-78623-901-3**

Dedication

This book is dedicated to the many wonderful volunteers who worked with Anne and I during our years of Children's, Youth and Adult Ministries in Londonderry, Inishown and on the Isle of Man.

And in memory of one special volunteer, our lovely daughter-in-law Karen, whom the Lord took home suddenly on the 10th May 2006

To God be the Glory

CHAPTER ONE

Every book, I'm told, needs an exciting, attention-catching opening phrase or sentence; I wish I had one! And many tales, especially fairy tales, begin with 'Once upon a time'. But, as this is no fairy tale, this true story really must begin with 'ONCE UPON AN EGG'! This egg, however, stirred up a memory that led to a ministry all of which was God inspired. The egg will have to wait until after introductions.

I am Roy, and at the time of this story I was working as an engineering supervisor for a large company a few miles outside my home city of Londonderry. I lived with my wife Anne, who was a midwife at the local hospital GP maternity unit, and our four children: Ian, our eldest son and Richard were both at grammar school, Adrian our youngest son and our daughter Karen were still at primary school. Our home was at No. 71 Irish Street, Londonderry.

Now let me bring the egg into the story, which begins on a Sunday morning in 1977. I had just taken the family off to Sunday school and church. Anne, following her night shift, was preparing for bed. As she looked out of the bedroom window she could see a number of neighbourhood children playing on the green opposite the house.

'Why,' she asked herself, 'are they not at Sunday school? Do the parents not attend church?'

Then, as she climbed into bed, she remembered... THE EGG.

Anne, or Annie as she was known, is a farmer's daughter, one of a family of six girls and two boys. Their farm was in Edymore, just outside Strabane, Co Tyrone. Each Sunday afternoon the children from the neighbourhood were invited to the home of Mrs Fulton, the wife of a local farmer. There, this lovely Christian lady taught a Sunday school with songs and Bible stories which Annie very clearly remembered. There was also the brown egg, which each child received on his or her birthday and at Easter.

Now Annie's family had hens and eggs, but these eggs were carefully washed, packed and sold to pay for the weekly groceries. Anyway, there was something rather special about receiving a brown egg from Mrs Fulton. Oh! By the way, in those days there were more white eggs than brown, so a brown egg was that bit more special. So, as Anne watched the children playing that Sunday morning, God began planting in her mind a plan that would bring glory to Him, and begin an evangelism explosion in the lives of thousands of children, youth and the elderly.

CHAPTER TWO

The year 1977 proved to be a dramatic and traumatic year for us. In January, at four years of age in Junior Christian Endeavour, Karen gave her life to the Lord. In March I was struck down with a viral illness that stopped me working for three months, and in June my dad, and mentor, died. However, having shared her brown egg story and vision with me, Anne and I felt compelled to do something, so we prayed for God's help and guidance.

The first step seemed very clear. We would open our home and have a Bible club for the children of the area. Invitations were given out for the children, with their parents' permission, to join 'A Children's Bible Club to be held each Tuesday evening at 6.30pm in Roy and Anne Porter's home, No. 71 Irish Street, Londonderry'.

The Bible club proved to be very popular and children from surrounding districts also joined. No brown eggs, but lots of biscuits and drinks accompanied the songs and Bible stories. So many children joined that the club became two, one meeting in the front room for the age group four to nine, and the other meeting in the back room for children aged ten to fourteen. Anne conducted the younger group, and I taught the older group. We were blessed with help from our family and other Christian friends.

One evening my cousin, Sharon, came to visit. She was at that time on the local Child Evangelism Fellowship (CEF) committee. She asked about our children's Bible club and then told us about the CEF programme of Good News Clubs. At her suggestion I contacted the local CEF director Roland Brown, who came and presented the CEF teaching programme which included flannelgraph lessons. Flannelgraph, the 'in' teaching tool of those days, had Bible stories with cut-out flock-backed figures and scenery which adhered to a felt-covered board, thus giving visual expression to the Bible lessons being taught. We adopted this new method and became officially part of the CEF programme. The Bible club became a Good News Club, the registered name for CEF Bible clubs. Songs and memory verses were hand-printed on card, and the Irish Street Good News Club was established. Also included as part of the programme was teacher training, conducted by Roland for Good News Club teachers.

The Good News Club season ran from September to Easter and some of the highlights were... the visits with the children to hospitals and nursing homes at Christmas to sing carols and chat with the patients, the end of season Good News Club rallies, and summer camp in either Castlerock or Portstewart. We were greatly helped by the local director Roland Brown, who asked me to join the committee responsible for overseeing the area work. Anne and I also attended the monthly area prayer meetings and helped in the youth work, summer camp and outreach. This greatly widened our knowledge about the overall work of the Child Evangelism Fellowship of Ireland and CEF worldwide.

Anne and I also had a singing ministry and, as duettists, we were invited to various meetings and conferences. On some of those occasions I was given the opportunity to speak about our role with CEF.

Anne writes:

'At this time Roy was still working with his company (sometimes day and night) and my three nights a week as a midwife were Thursday, Friday and Saturday. I still remember the joy of coming home on Friday morning, filling and placing my hot water bottle in bed and taking the children to school in my wee yellow mini – especially in the winter. I must admit it was a great feeling watching everyone facing the elements on their way to work knowing I was going home to a nice warm bed.

'I'd set the alarm for 3.15pm at which time I was off to school again to pick up the children. Not so much joy now of course as it was overseeing homework and preparing dinner, but on Saturdays and Sundays Roy was in charge. His Saturday specialty was mince stew cooked in a pressure cooker and with baked beans added later. On one occasion when I was available I cooked something different, which was greeted with a chorus of, "Oh, where's the stew?"

'This was the pattern for seven years, and during this time we began our voluntary CEF involvement. Firstly, opening our home for a Good News Club, then accepting an invitation from a couple in a local housing estate to come and teach their children. This couple had only recently become Christians; they had in their family two adopted and three fostered children. This became a fully-fledged Good News Club with over 40 attending, and the teaching also proved beneficial to the parents.

'I then had a call for help from my friend Joan, who had a late afternoon Good News Club in the Lismacarol Mission

Hall, located in the village of Drumahoe, a few miles outside Londonderry. I remember taking my flannelgraph lesson book into work and, during quiet spells, cutting out the flock-backed figures. During our tea breaks I would practise my lesson on my colleague, Rose, who was a devout Roman Catholic but who knew little of the Bible. She really enjoyed hearing about the Life of David, the Acts of the Apostles etc. She asked many questions and one night asked what the Bible said about St Patrick! She and I still keep in touch, but now our main topics are aches, pains and families, although in my letters I try to encourage her in spiritual matters.'

. . . .

When Roland resigned from CEF to take up a teaching post in the technical college, Anne and I became more and more involved in the local work. With the two clubs in our home, Anne teaching and helping in the Good News Club at the local Mission Hall, and both of us now involved in the home of the Christian couple, we were teaching four Good News Clubs. We were still helping in the youth programme, summer outreach and camp. Thankfully, we kept plenty of time for our family, but something had to give! So next came the proposal:

The scene - our bedroom in Irish Street; it is April 1982 at 2.30pm. I had been to a funeral and before returning to work I woke Anne bearing a cup of tea.

'Hello sweetheart,' I began, 'I want to share something with you. I believe that God would have me, and perhaps even us, leave our employment and take up a full-time Christian ministry.'

She reminded me that she had a headache and chased me back to work.

Chapter Two

Later that day we prayed together, and I told her that my company was offering a package for senior staff to take early retirement. Although I didn't qualify, we decided that I should apply. When attempts to dissuade me failed, my application was accepted and I was included in the package. Our God working things out as only He can. But to do what? And with whom? So I sent for information from various missionary organisations, and Anne and I even visited their representatives but we had no peace regarding any of these.

In our home we had a world globe money bank furnished by CEF for missionary offerings; these were collected biannually by committee members. It was time for the spring collection and two of our committee members, Rona Taylor and Heather Smyth, arrived to visit. Over a cup of tea, we shared with them what we felt God calling us to do.

'Have you not considered CEF?' said Rona. 'Roland resigning has opened the door for new directors.'

We were stunned. Why hadn't we thought about the very mission we were volunteers with? Suddenly, the peace we had been missing came flooding in. Together with our committee friends we prayed, and that very evening I contacted Roland about the possibility of full-time CEF directorship. Roland was delighted; he contacted the national CEF director, and he, also delighted, arranged for Anne and me to visit the National Office that very week.

The national directors were David and Molly McQuilken; it was David who interviewed us and gave us forms to fill in. We talked about Bible college, but David decided that my Bible college correspondence courses would meet the criteria. He then enrolled us in the Leadership Training Programme at the CEF European Headquarters in Kilchzimmer, Switzerland.

WOW! Things were moving fast.

Chapter Three

Once accepted for Kilchzimmer, we handed in our resignations and sold our two old cars (oh! how Anne struggled parting with her little yellow mini, but that's another story). Thanks to the package from the company and savings, we were able to buy a new car and fund our passage to Europe. Richard had now finished college and was waiting to go to university; Ian was living and studying in Bangor. So, taking Adrian and Karen with us, we headed off at the end of June to the CEF Institute in Switzerland.

CEF of Europe had taken over and refurbished an old nunnery up in the Jura Mountains of northern Switzerland, and there we spent our summer and part of the autumn in training. The Lord really undertook for us during this period, especially for Anne and the kids. Back in Londonderry Richard was living in our home, and kept an eye on by a Christian neighbour, whose son was Richard's close friend.

During our time at the institute, Adrian became very involved in the printing department, packing banana boxes with teaching materials for distribution throughout eastern Europe. It kept him out of mischief and spared the hens his rooster calls. He, of course, was treated as staff and enjoyed meals with his adult colleagues, including the European national director! Karen had been given past exam papers to look over in preparation for her forthcoming transfer test (the result of this test would determine whether or not she would go to grammar school. On her return from Switzerland she sat and passed the test).

Our time in Switzerland was both enlightening and exhausting, mentally, physically and emotionally. The latter was especially true for those with English or French as their second language. The classes were composed of various nationalities and everyone got on extremely well. The morning began with chores then prayer meetings, which were taken by students who would read a scripture and give a short devotional thought. Each morning various subjects relating to scripture, children's ministry and leadership etc. were taught. Lunch and quiet hour came next, then a free afternoon of games, usually volleyball, walking and for some, especially the ladies, shopping.

There was one incident which became, for me, the subject of a sermon. It was games time, and I with some other students and lecturers played volleyball in glorious sunshine. Anne and some of the ladies were taken by minibus into the village in the valley town. Some time later when we had finished our games and were sitting enjoying the sunshine, the minibus returned and had evidently driven through rain; the ladies alighted with their coats quite wet. We, of course, had played volleyball above a low rain cloud; the ladies weren't so fortunate. Months later, thinking back on this incident, I used it when preparing a sermon on the Mount of Transfiguration. I was led to consider the contrast between the disciples Peter, James and John witnessing the glorified Jesus on the mountain, and the other disciples in the valley failing to cure the epileptic boy. Glory on the mountain, heartache in the valley until, that is, Jesus entered the scene and brought healing and restoration. Praise God, in life's valleys, Jesus still does that today.

There were enjoyable outings by bus, walks to the ice cream parlour and games in the upstairs room on Saturday evenings. We also enjoyed great times of spiritual fellowship on Sundays, and quiet times of refreshing, but then there were emotional moments such as when plans were made to travel to the American soldiers' camp in Germany. Usually all the students and families went but this year accommodation was scarce, so only the menfolk went. This was not well-received by some of the wives; one cried and exclaimed that she had never been separated from seeing her husband all their married life. Anne didn't mind too much (she said) as I and the men headed off to hold Five Day Clubs with the army children.

I was billeted with a lovely American family in whose home the coffee pot never cooled. On the Sunday morning of our time there, I was asked by the church padre to take the Sunday school. So, carrying a folder of teaching materials, I entered the church hall to find that the Sunday school was for adults! However, with a quick prayer I gathered my thoughts, and was able to conduct an acceptable class using a bit of my CEF background and a devotional I had prepared for a teacher training class as part of the institute training.

Close to completing our course, Anne had the unfortunate experience of falling downstairs and tearing ligaments in her left leg. On advice she declined an operation in Switzerland, so she attended graduation wearing a knee length plaster of Paris.

Back home, having been interviewed and accepted by the CEF National Committee, we prepared for ministry as local CEF directors in our home area of north-west Ulster. The Commissioning Service was to be held in our local church, Ebrington Presbyterian. Anne was determined she was not going to the front wearing a plaster, so at the local hospital she prayed fervently for healing. The plaster was removed, her leg was X-rayed and no ligament damage was found; not even scar tissue, even though Anne had the Swiss X-rays with her which showed ligament damage. So Anne walked down the church aisle plaster free. 'I am the God that healeth thee' Exodus 15:26 (AV). Later on this verse was to play a major role in my life.

The Reverend Bill Addley, our minister, conducted the service and the CEF of Ireland fieldworker, Kenneth Martin, gave what is known as 'the charge' to Anne and I as missionaries. Kenneth was later to be a regular visitor to our Londonderry home during our first year of ministry. He conducted teacher training evenings and attended our committee meetings, giving us the benefit of his vast experience.

CHAPTER FOUR

Over the next seven years the Lord enabled the work in north-west Ulster to grow. Earlier the teacher training programme was referred to; this was now an essential part of the ministry as clubs opened in Londonderry, Eglinton, Limavady, Dungiven and Inishowen, Co Donegal. In all, by 1987 the area had 40 Good News Clubs with around 100 volunteer teachers and helpers. Teacher training classes were held in Londonderry, Limavady and Dungiven; the teachers from Donegal travelled to Londonderry. I, sometimes accompanied by Anne, travelled many miles throughout the area and into Inishowen, conducting school assemblies; some of these were long enough for a mini Good News Club programme.

We had many wonderful volunteers who assisted us with our various clubs. I want to mention two in particular who today are still great friends, encouragers and supporters. And do I mind if they care about me mentioning them? Not at all. That is the depth of our friendship.

Anne and I met Alistair Campbell at our first CEF promotional meeting held in a church hall just outside Dungiven.

Chapter Four

In trepidation we stood before the assembled congregation who had come to meet and hear us. I opened the meeting with a scripture reading and prayer, and then, just as Anne was about to talk about our ministry, the door opened. A tall and bearded young gentleman entered, apologised and took a seat at the back. Not a bit disconcerted, Anne launched into her spiel; I was very proud of her and she spoke well. I closed with a short message from scripture and, of course, we had tea etc. The tall and bearded young gentleman approached me and introduced himself:

'Hello, my name is Alistair Campbell and I am a school teacher. I have been to New Zealand and met with some CEF workers there. When I heard about this meeting I wanted to come and meet you.'

This meeting led to a friendship with one who would later prove to be an exceptional volunteer worker, committee member and camp officer.

At this same meeting while I was talking to Alistair, an elderly lady approached Anne.

'My name is Mrs Bunn,' she said 'I was a school teacher and my husband was a headmaster. Now I am thrilled at what you are doing for the children, but you also said you had four children of your own. The questions I want to ask are, "Where are they tonight and who is looking after them?" Just remember they are the ones that God gave you and must take priority.'

This may seem quite blunt but Anne did not take offence. She assured Mrs Bunn that our children were well looked after in our absence and did have first priority in our lives. Mrs Bunn became a firm friend in the ensuing years and Anne and I visited her often, usually for morning tea which was always served in china cups. She eventually sold her home and moved into the Cornfield Care Centre just outside Limavady.

Anne and I visited her there but she didn't know or remember us. Shortly after that she went home to be with her Lord and saviour.

Now let me introduce another friend, Fred Corscadden, who himself was introduced to us by the aforementioned Alistair. The introduction took place at one of our first teacher training evenings in Limavady. Following the training programme I asked our newcomer, Fred, to close in prayer, not knowing that I was asking Fred, a young Christian, to pray for the first time in public. The Lord certainly helped him for he closed the meeting with a very relevant prayer. Fred became another very close friend and associate, volunteer and camp officer. Again these are just two of a host of amazing people without whom the work in north-west Ulster could not have expanded.

Although the winter ministries began in October, the area held an annual dinner each November to introduce those involved in the area ministry, at which I would give an annual report. This also included musical items and a closing address usually given by the CEF national or international directors.

Good News Club (GNC) rallies were held at the end of each winter season in Londonderry and Limavady, and were a highlight of the GNC programme. At these the finals of the area's GNC quiz were held, when the three chosen finalists competed for the GNC shields.

The summer GNC camp was held during the first week in July, usually in either the Castlerock or Portstewart primary schools. Greatly anticipated and well-attended, this was always a week of great fun, food and fellowship. Over 60 campers enjoyed excellent Bible teaching, missionary stories and very special evening quiet times in their dormitories. There were fun evenings which included a fancy dress and concert, and also an afternoon of 'hunt the worker' when the leaders dressed up in various outfits and waited in the town for the campers to find and recognise them. One of the leaders, with permission, dressed in a butcher's apron and stood in the butcher's shop pretending to work. There were would-be car mechanics, window cleaners and some elderly ladies were amazed and delighted to be shown across the road by what we call a 'lollipop person', complete with pole. Their comment: 'and in July too, with the schools closed, how thoughtful'.

William, another leader, donned a clerical collar but was soon recognised by a group of campers who dashed up to him with the prearranged question. A lady standing nearby scolded the group, saying, 'Stop that and leave the reverend alone.' William embarrassingly explained what was happening. In Portstewart there was a convent and nuns were regularly seen about town. During a game of 'hunt the worker', a nun was approached and stood in astonishment as she was surrounded by a noisy group of campers! Fortunately, one of our leaders (we always had a non-participating leader on patrol) was able to move in and explain the situation. The nun was greatly amused and congratulated the children on being very observant. None of the leaders was, on this occasion, dressed as a nun.

As numbers grew the camp became two camps; one for the juniors and another for the seniors. The junior camp met one week, Monday to Friday, then the team rested on Saturday and Sunday before beginning again on Sunday evening with the senior camp. One very welcome camp member was our dog, Sparky; there was no shortage of volunteers to take him on his daily walks.

Our cook was very fond of using baked beans with the dinners, especially when she made her runny mince. One evening after the younger children had settled down for the night, there was a commotion in the corridor. One of the campers, on his mattress, had been dragged out from the dorm. He was in tears when Anne got to him. She took him and his mattress back into the dorm and asked, 'What is the cause of all this commotion?' only to be told that the unfortunate camper had been passing wind!

'Please Anne,' said one of the other dorm inhabitants, 'don't let cook give him any more baked beans.'

Suppressing a smile, Anne gathered the children together and said, 'Let's pray about it'. What followed was a lovely time of prayer and reconciliation. I might add that the dorm leader, who shall remain nameless, had switched off his hearing aid and had blissfully slept through the activities; or so he said, trying to conceal a grin.

With many of the former GNC children now teenagers, a new CEF group was formed. This group was named 'Junior Youth Challenge'. Here the programme was geared to an 11 to 13-year-old age group led by our friend Don Rowan and, as this group grew older, a 'Senior Youth Challenge' group was created for children aged 14 and over. This senior group was led by another supporter and former GNC teacher, Matt Dinsmore. How we praised God for faithful leaders and teachers.

The young people always looked forward to the Youth Challenge weekends usually held in Carrigart, Co Donegal. In those early days our venue was an unused Presbyterian manse, available for hire. The house had no heating and was certainly not draughtproof. The lounge/meeting room had a log-fuelled fire and on one occasion, when Roland Brown was the guest speaker at a senior weekend, he volunteered to sleep in the lounge and keep the fire burning. At about midnight, Anne and I were wakened by the sound of slithering and sliding on the stairs and in the corridors. On investigation we discovered that the senior boys, together with their leaders, and with their mattresses, had decided to join Roland. I was so sorry I didn't have my camera with me. We just smiled, shook our heads and returned to bed.

I recall on another Youth Challenge weekend, our speakers were Chris and Jennifer Haaijer. At that time they were overseeing the CEF work in the Ukraine. The young people were thrilled as Chris reported on the ministry there, and Anne and I were thrilled as Jennifer taught on the Beatitudes. How much those young people must have learned that weekend on mission and from the Bible. Anne and I, the leaders and the young people enjoyed many memorable weekends first in Donegal and later in Portrush, Co Antrim.

It was at one of those weekends that Paul and Karen Sayers, now living in the Isle of Man, first met and fell in love; more of Paul and Karen later. Another young couple, Gavin Boyd and Julie Norris, also met at a senior weekend; they are now married and leading a church in Gran Canaria, one of the Canary Islands. Peter Rowan, son of Don and May, is now director of the Overseas Missionary Fellowship. Sean Adair is in the Methodist ministry and Adrian Porter pastors a church in the Isle of Man (more of him later). These are just a few of the many former CEF-related young people who are involved either in full-time or church-related ministries. Thanks be to our amazing God!

Invitations were often given for Anne and me to visit churches and church groups to speak about the ministry. CEF were grateful for the practical and financial support received. Up to now finances have not been mentioned, but the northwest Ulster area, as with other CEF areas, was autonomous. Finances were raised locally and used to support the local work, as well as helping to meet the needs at National Office. The committee met once a month in the new office which Anne and I had built beside our home using our personal finances. Here we prayed and discussed future programmes and the building up of financial support. One of our committee members produced an income versus outgoings graph, and wonderfully we never had too much but we were always 'in the black'. Anne and I, as local directors, received our salary from the area account. We also attended the Irish CEF staff conferences in Kilkeel, Easter conferences in Portrush, and European conferences in Denmark and Germany.

When the Reverend Bill Addley accepted a ministerial teaching position in Brazil, our home church was seeking a replacement. During the vacancy I, with other elders, shared the preaching in the evening services. I was also invited to take services in Donegal churches which were linked to churches in Londonderry. At times I would conduct and preach in three services on a Sunday morning, all starting just over an hour apart; there was no time for handshakes at the doors after the first and second services. This was an enjoyable and privileged part of my extra ministry.

There were numerous other ministries in which Anne and I were involved and where our CEF experience helped. We were invited by many churches to demonstrate our CEF teaching materials and hold Sunday school teacher training days. These were held on Saturdays and began with the demonstration and use of CEF materials, but the main purpose, at least that is what I felt, was to help teachers use their own Sunday school materials more effectively. This part of the programme was conducted in the morning, followed by lunch. Then, in the afternoon, we held a session of more practical help with teacher involvement.

Our local church asked us to take over the 'Bright Hour', a weekly programme of scones and tea, singing well-known hymns and finishing with a simple, sometimes illustrated, Bible message. This was for our senior citizens among others, who loved those times of food and fellowship.

In association with William and Sandra Workman, who were at that time working with the Londonderry City Mission, Anne and I conducted an afternoon Sunday school in the YMCA hall at Drumahoe, Londonderry.

In Limavady, some Christian friends, two of whom were on the CEF committee, were challenged regarding the opening of a drop-in centre on the outskirts of the town. There was already a hall there which had been built and used by another mission, and which the drop-in group had permission to use. Anne and I also became involved with helping in the drop-in, especially with the spiritual side of the ministry.

We were also Sunday school teachers in our own church and I was responsible for the teaching programme; for this we used Scripture Press material. Scripture Press was an organisation with close links to CEF. Both organisations joined together to hold yearly teaching conferences. I didn't stick to the Scripture Press weekly programme but divided the lessons into six weekly sections separated by an open Sunday school, during which the past lessons were reviewed by means of a quiz. Don and May Rowan, also Sunday school teachers, featured a great deal in the CEF ministry, especially in the Junior Youth Challenge where Don was the leader. They also helped us with our Summer Outreach Programme.

An accomplished guitarist, our eldest son, Ian, helped with music in various events; most memorable was at an outreach in Buncrana, Co Donegal. Although north-west Ulster CEF was officially based in Northern Ireland, we had many connections across the 'Border' especially in Inishowen. One of our committee members, Hillary Lamberton, whose husband and family were farmers in Inishowen, asked for help in setting up a Christian outreach in Buncrana as the town was hosting 'the Fleadh'; a South of Ireland Festival. With a great spot on the main street we set up a public address system, sang

Christian songs and shared testimonies. I had the privilege not only of conducting the proceedings but also giving a short Bible message. The group then gave out Bible tracts during the procession.

Ian remembers with, he says, some embarrassment, his mum and me making a tape in which I sang the opening song using a recording of him playing guitar as the accompaniment; I must admit to feeling slightly embarrassed myself. The rest of our songs were accompanied by Joan Lynch playing the organ. The idea for the tape came from our friend, Gary Ming, who also managed the recording, which was made in the Lismacarol Mission Hall. The tape, although it was a great hit with Anne's family and friends at home, in Scotland, in Australia and in New Zealand, never quite made the top ten.

On another occasion Ian also contributed, inadvertently, to the CEF ministry in north-west Ulster by allowing me to have his guitar. At the time Ian was living in Newtownards and had married Margaret. One day his precious twelve-stringed Yamaha guitar had an accident, and suffered a broken neck. Ian used to busk for charity in Belfast and I think the accident happened when he fell off his motorbike on the way home. Not to be outdone, Ian screwed and glued the broken bits together and restrung the Yamaha. However, it was only possible to use six strings in order to protect the neck of the guitar. Ian therefore needed a new guitar, so I contributed to the cost and became the proud owner of a now six-stringed Yamaha guitar. Although I couldn't play, our daughter Karen used the Yamaha on many occasions. I might add here that before going off to university Karen had instructed me in the rudiments of guitar playing and all I needed was practice.

Prior to the end of the school year I was asked to speak at high school and grammar school Scripture Unions. Here I met and recruited a number of young folk to take part in the various ministries of CEF, winter and summer. To be a part of this ministry, volunteers of 16 years and upwards were sent for training to the CEF Centre in Kilkeel, Co Down. They then returned and put into practice what they had learned, teaching in Five Day and Holiday Bible Clubs as part of, or sometimes leading, Summer Outreach Teams.

To promote the forthcoming Summer Outreach Programme, each May a 'Praise Evening' was held, usually in one of the local primary schools. With this Anne and I were blessed with help from our church choir led by Jaqueline Tosh, musical items from a selection of Senior Youth Challenge members and summer missionaries, usually organised by Karen, and a guest speaker who would give a challenge to 'go and tell'. Area prayer partners and supporters of our work were invited, the planned summer programme was introduced, and the evening ended with the usual tea, sandwiches and cakes.

The CEF summer programme consisted of Five Day Clubs which, as the name suggests, were clubs held in the open air for five days lasting one hour, in as many areas as we could possibly manage. Here the aforementioned Don, who played accordion, and May with her wonderful singing voice, led the music.

The years when our north-west area summer programmes took place were during the period known as 'the Troubles', and Anne and I, with our summer missionaries, entered some areas with trepidation. In one such area we were interrupted, just as Anne was teaching on Paul on the road to Damascus, by a group of menacing-looking teenagers. They walked through the group of children causing some to leave, and then off they went without threatening us. We told the rest of the children to go home but promised we would return the following evening. Later that evening we prayed for God to intervene. The next evening we did return, but noticed one of our team had arrived carrying a large bag. Anne later learned she had in her bag a small baseball bat and helmet; thankfully they weren't needed but it made Anne, and me, smile.

As we were preparing for our meeting we noticed a group of mothers standing nearby. They had brought their children and others with them to our meeting, but before leaving one of the mothers told us we were not to worry about what had happened on the previous evening, and that they were just glad we were not canvassing for the IRA. Since that time many clubs have been held in that area, and in other such areas, without disturbance.

Some clubs presented the outreach teams with other problems. At one club a few older children gathered worms and, during the meeting, rushed over and put them down the necks of the seated team members. Another club was interrupted when teenagers wielding gorse branches chased the summer missionaries from their area, but our team were not to be discouraged. After praying for God's help they returned the next evening, and to this day that club has continued without interference. Praise be to our intervening, wonderful God!

The other summer ministry of Holiday Bible Clubs were clubs which were again held for five days but for two and a half hours, often in church halls and with church sponsorship, but also in other places, hired or granted, including games and workbooks. This meant many hours of travelling and teaching, but Anne and I and our teams felt truly blessed.

Anne and I also organised Holiday Bible Clubs in Inishowen, Co Donegal; this was in association with our Good News Club teachers in the Inishowen area of Muff. We were invited to hold a club in the Presbyterian church hall in Malin, also in Inishowen. It was well-received and the following year we were asked to go again. To avoid Anne and I having to travel each day, the thoughtful Malin church members installed us in a guest house during the week of Holiday Bible Club. Wow! That was like a week of holiday because, with the club being held in the evening, Anne and I had all day to explore the beautiful Malin district. This, we knew, was what the lovely people of Malin had intended.

One highlight of the summer, and not CEF-related, were the weekly open-air meetings held in as many housing estates as could be fitted in. Anne and I enjoyed taking part when available, as members of our church outreach team. For all of the open-air meetings the church book trailer was used, which had a public address (PA) system. We didn't sell many books but reached hundreds of adults and young ones through songs, testimonies and Bible messages.

Anne and I also took our Senior Youth Challenge group to church halls and borrowed caravans, which we used for a week of Bible studies for the group. We used this opportunity to hold Holiday Bible Clubs and Five Day Clubs with children at various venues. Also included were evening outreaches to adults; for these we were grateful for the use of the book trolley 'PA'.

Another highlight was the end-of-summer report evening which included a fork supper, namely a meat or chicken dish with rice. These evenings were very popular, and well-attended by many summer workers and prayer partners to hear the summer missionaries reporting on their adventures. Blessed days!

Anne and I introduced the telephone ministry in north-west Ulster in the mid-1980s. John and Joan Nixon, CEF missionaries in Cork, Southern Ireland, had used this ministry for many years and now Northern Ireland was using it. A Bible message was recorded onto an answering machine tape and the telephone number was widely advertised throughout the area. The children and some adults would listen to the message, then leave their name and address. Bible booklets and New Testaments were then sent out to the callers. Many children came to faith in Christ through this ministry. Anne also looked after the correspondence course, another great outreach and follow up ministry.

The telephone ministry had many wonderful stories attached to it but this one I want to share. 'J' had been saved through Good News Club and later became involved with Youth Challenge. She had regularly listened to the telephone message and received many booklets. On one occasion Anne, who at this early stage was listening and responding to the numerous callers, recognised J's voice. She asked Anne to send her a Bible and booklet for her friend Elizabeth, which Anne duly did. Anne heard nothing more about Elizabeth until the following Easter conference in Portrush. There she read in a local newspaper about a road crash on the Glenshane Pass part of the Londonderry to Belfast route. In one of the cars a grandmother, mother and daughter were fatally injured. The daughter was J from the telephone ministry, the mother was... Elizabeth.

So many wonderful memories; so many amazing experiences and so wonderful to look back on how the Lord worked and blessed during our time with CEF in north-west Ulster.

CHAPTER FIVE

After what had been a very busy 1987 summer programme Anne and I were exhausted, so Richard decided we needed a break without the family. He would look after Adrian, Karen and home while we took off for a holiday. After checking our finances, we discovered a holiday in the Isle of Man was affordable so, taking no car, we set sail with the Steam Packet ferry and enjoyed a lovely Indian summer break. We stayed in a guest house in Douglas and also took in some bus journeys during which we saw most of the Island.

On the Sunday we worshipped at Broadway Baptist Church where a young Irishman, David Gordon, was the pastor. After the evening service and, of course, over a cup of tea, we introduced ourselves and told him how we came to be there. David knew of CEF having attended some of their open-air meetings in his home town of Bangor, Co Down. He wondered if it would be possible for us to take over an outreach team the following summer as there were a number of areas on the Island where children, and perhaps even adults, knew little or nothing of the Bible stories; most may never even have heard a gospel message. We told him we would discuss it with our committee and let him know. The committee agreed to Anne and I planning an outreach, but perhaps later in the summer when our other work was complete.

It was then time for Adrian to go to university, so Anne and I took him to the airport where Anne tried her best to hide a tear. For the next five years Adrian would study engineering at Napier College, just outside Edinburgh. Napier was soon to become a part of Edinburgh University.

I mentioned Paul and Karen Sayers earlier. Paul worked in a bank in Londonderry but lived in Strabane. His family were known to Anne, and she was asked to feed him on the day he attended the Londonderry Technical College. Paul was familiar with the work of CEF having taught in Five Day Clubs in the Strabane Area. Karen Peters (as she was then called) was a recruit to CEF from my Scripture Union (SU) visits. She also taught a Good News Club in her home in Ballykelly, near Limavady, and had worked with us in many of our summer outreaches. Paul had provided the music for us at one or two of our Senior Youth Challenge weekends and, as previously mentioned, it was at one such a weekend that love blossomed. Karen and Paul eventually married; Anne and I sang at their wedding.

They both came to our home one evening to share something with us. This was when we were being challenged about the Isle of Man outreach. They knew nothing about our association with the Isle of Man, so they couldn't understand why Anne and I smiled broadly on hearing that Paul had been offered a job in a branch of his bank in the Isle of Man. We told them we were delighted, and then shared with them our own plans regarding the possible Isle of Man outreach. Paul and Karen went to live in the Isle of Man in January 1988.

In the spring of that year Broadway Baptist Church financed a weekend trip for Anne and me to again visit the Isle of Man, staying this time with an Irish couple, Hillary and Russell Hamilton, in their Douglas guest house. The purpose of this trip was to speak with supportive Christians and possible summer workers invited by David Gordon, and to give an overview of what the summer outreach would entail. We also showed a sample of the teaching materials, invitations and follow-up booklets used in summer outreach programmes.

On our return, Anne and I set about selecting a team of experienced summer workers, then in August 1988, with our part in the north-west Ulster summer programme complete, we sailed on a rather uncomfortable sea to the Isle of Man. A few of the team were a little sick but we survived the voyage. The meeting with Pastor David Gordon was encouraging. He had made out a list of areas which he felt would benefit from the outreach. However, Richard and Gavin were aghast to learn that the following Sunday they were scheduled to preach at Baptist and Independent Fellowship Churches. Team members Adrian and Doreen Walker were booked to sing and testify at the Ramsey Elim Church. Of those who were involved in that Sunday programme two are now pastors, written about earlier; Adrian in the Living Hope Community Church in the Isle of Man (how this came about is covered in a later chapter) and Gavin, who, with his wife Julie, pastors The International Evangelical Church in Gran Canaria.

With a number of Broadway and other church members involved, on Sunday afternoon invitations were given out in several areas. The week's programme included morning Holiday Bible Clubs, and afternoon and evening Five Day Clubs.

One poignant but amusing episode happened as one of the volunteer drivers offered to provide transport for three of the female members of the summer outreach team. As they arrived at his car the driver, Brian Gault, took the car key from his shoe, and with his right foot he opened the car doors for his passengers. Their amazement was evident but Brian assured them he was able to drive with his feet, and so, gingerly but bravely, they got into the car. Brian, true to his word, drove the young ladies to their destination. Brian, a member of Broadway Baptist Church, was one of the survivors of the so-called miracle drug thalidomide, and was born with no arms. His story, in his book 'Look No Hands', is well worth a read.

The members of the team from Northern Ireland were billeted with wonderful families in different parts of the Island. The couple with whom Anne and I stayed were our young friends Paul and Karen Sayers, who were now firmly settled and working in Douglas. As well as providing lodgings for one of the girls on the team, the local policeman, Graham, had a great challenge for the areas of Pulrose and Anagh Coar. It was the children of the area known as Pulrose, where we led and taught a Holiday Bible Club, who left the greatest impression on Anne and me. At that time there were quite a number of dysfunctional families living in that area, but they had lovely children. Later, when we learned that there would be a boat at Halloween, we arranged with Graham to have a reunion in Pulrose.

It had been a hectic and exhausting time of ministry but we and the team went back to Ireland with many happy memories, knowing that, during the outreach, a number of children and young people had been counselled for salvation.

Back again in north-west Ulster Anne and I were soon involved in our own ministries of Good News Clubs, teacher training and Youth Challenge etc. The work here was continuing to grow, with more homes opening for GNCs, and schools holding Harvest assemblies and, in December, Christmas clubs.

Chapter Five

Each September CEF held a conference in Kilkeel, Co Down. All the local area directors and available CEF missionaries attended. During one of the lunch breaks I got talking to a colleague, Robert Lacey. Robert and his wife, Irene, were local directors in South Antrim. I told him of our trip to the Isle of Man and of the outreach programme we had held there. He mentioned that he and Irene were planning a holiday on the Island next summer. At this my heart leapt! As God had done for us would He bring someone into contact with them regarding the spiritual needs of the Island's children? Anne and I committed the possibility to God in prayer, only to learn later that Robert and Irene's plans had changed when they were offered a holiday in Denmark. A closed door, or was another door opening, not necessarily for Robert and Irene, but for someone else?

With the north-west Ulster CEF winter programme up and running, Anne and I turned our thoughts to planning the Halloween reunion in the Isle of Man. Relevant to this is our son Ian's ability to conquer the shopping centre 'grab a cuddly toy' machine. He had over 100 of the lovely little toys, and when he heard of our Isle of Man reunion plan he arrived from Bangor with two plastic bags of 'cuddlies'. So Anne and I sailed once more to the Isle of Man eager to renew our acquaintance with the Pulrose children and adults.

On the afternoon prior to the reunion Bible Club we met in the police house with several other people, most of whom we didn't know. Graham had a chart on the wall with the first names of adults and children. He shared some distressing stories about the effect of witchcraft in the Island (things which I couldn't share in this narrative). We prayed at length concerning these matters, then prayer went up for the Bible Club. Later we met with those who would help in the club that evening and prayed again. 80 children attended the club and listened well to the Bible lesson, and each child left with a Bible booklet and a cuddly toy. We had many names and addresses to follow up. That night, as Anne and I travelled home on the late boat, we both knew that the Isle of Man was in God's plan for our future ministry.

Once back home we and the committee were soon busy preparing for Youth Challenge weekends in February, and GNC rallies in March and April. Then, later in the year, more preparation, this time for camp and summer outreach.

Anne wrote to David Gordon asking for information about the evangelical witness on the Isle of Man, Sunday schools and school assemblies. David replied with a very detailed letter summarising his thoughts and impressions regarding the spiritual condition, especially with regards to the Island's children. His investigations showed that although there were many good Sunday schools, many had ceased to function or were short of teachers and children. Very little spiritual teaching was used in school assemblies, and evangelical churches were few and far between, both geographically and doctrinally. On reading this comprehensive account, Anne and I were more than ever convinced that the Isle of Man was to be our next place of ministry.

The committee decided we should attend the 1988 European Conference being held that year in Denmark. Anne and I met up at Belfast airport with Kenneth Martin and some other CEF directors, along with a young friend of Kenneth's who, although suffering with MS, was very keen to travel to the conference. It was an excellent conference with many interesting reports and challenging Bible messages. It was good, too, to meet up with many of the European CEF missionaries and directors. Anne and I were even invited to the platform to sing 'How great Thou art'.

Chapter Five

It was when we were homeward bound that things went, as they say, pear-shaped! We caught the train in Denmark and travelled to Germany where we were to be met by the local CEF workers. Somehow we managed to alight at the wrong station, and what a station it looked to be as it was occupied by some unsavoury looking characters, male and female. After much confusion it was decided that we should book into a hotel. David organised this and we all withdrew money from the ATM. David jokingly told Anne, 'Sorry Anne, we couldn't get separate rooms so you'll have to bunk in with the boys.' Anne told him she was so tired she didn't care. We laughed and headed for the hotel; Anne and I had a separate room. A couple of taxis were hired the next morning and we were off to the airport. Quite an adventure.

Anne and I planned to move to the Isle of Man once the 1989 summer ministry in north-west Ulster had been completed so, during the period from April to June, much preparation was needed, and we still had summer outreach and camp to organise. On checking the Isle of Man High School curriculum, we discovered that our daughter Karen would need to repeat her lower sixth year. When Karen was informed of this her response was, 'No way, there isn't any way that God would want me to repeat my lower sixth year,' and she stormed upstairs to her bedroom. This came as a blow to our plans, but we had underestimated God, and our very spiritual daughter. After a short time, Karen reappeared downstairs and hugged us both. She told us that having prayed through the situation with God, she now felt that nothing should stand in the way of His plan, so repeating her lower sixth it would be. This decision would prove to be amazing with regards to our early days in the Isle of Man. Through her own very special ministry of encouragement, many young teens would come into contact with her Lord Jesus Christ. This was all the encouragement we needed, although our son Richard was not convinced about our move. He thought that perhaps we were too old for what he felt would be a very demanding ministry. However, he was willing, although reluctantly, to support us.

With this new encouragement we put our house on the market, but although we had some viewers, the prices being offered were well below our expectations. Our house was situated between two contrasting areas, Nationalist, even Republican, on one side and Unionist Protestant on the other. As our estate agent said, 'If this house was located in any other quiet area it would fetch twice as much as is being offered.' There were indeed many occasions when opposing factions met up close to where we lived with resulting violence, thankfully not to us.

On one occasion when Anne and I, along with Adrian, Karen and a young lady named Ruth, the daughter of a clergyman, were visiting in Donegal, trouble was brewing in our neighbourhood. The young lady's father was not too sure about her coming to work with us in trouble-filled 'Derry', but we assured him things were not too bad where we lived. Just as we arrived home that evening and I had parked the car in our driveway, Adrian spotted a number of hooded lads coming towards the housing estate opposite.

'It's the Fenians!' he cried.

The group began to hurl petrol bombs at the parked cars in the estate opposite our house. One landed on the grass between the estate and our road, so Adrian decided to run over and kick the offending item back towards the advancing group. Fortunately, and thankfully, the perpetrators of the violence didn't seem to notice, so Adrian was roughly rescued by me and dragged from the scene. Meanwhile Anne, Karen and Ruth ran into the house where Ruth immediately phoned for the police to come. Needless to say Ruth enjoyed the excitement but didn't tell her father.

We were further encouraged with our Isle of Man plans when we learned from Paul and Karen that Fiona Biggart, a high school teacher who lived at No. 18 Windsor Road in Douglas, was leaving the Island on a year's secondment to another college. Anne and I had planned another quick visit to the Isle of Man to look at house prices, so we took our car over as soon as the spring sailings started. We stayed again with Paul and Karen, and on our first evening there I headed off to speak to Fiona. Anne and I had known Fiona from our previous visits to the Island, but I wasn't aware that many folks on the Isle of Man went early to bed, so at 9.30pm when I arrived at her home, she greeted me wearing her dressing gown. I apologised, explained the reason for my visit, and there and then she said she would be delighted to have us come and live in her house during her absence. Details could be sorted out later... goodnight!

Now the time had come to share with the local committee so, at the next committee meeting, we told the members about what we strongly felt was our new calling. 'Flabbergasted' sums up the reaction as we shared our vision, but after some discussion it was obvious to the members that this was the will of God. We then asked permission to go back again to the Isle of Man to talk with some church leaders and other Christians. It was agreed that we could go in March at the end of the winter activities.

Next we contacted our national directors David and Molly McQuilken. While speaking with them, David shared with us an outreach he had been involved in on the Isle of Man many years previously, and he still had a soft spot for the Island. He also confided in us that he had been working on a plan to create Armagh as the training area for new workers and had us in mind for the position of directors there; as things turned out this plan never came to fruition. We also told David we believed that God would have the Isle of Man ministry autonomous, and no finances would come from our area contacts. We returned home quite encouraged.

When we spoke with Sam Doherty, the CEF European director, his reaction was:

'Why the Isle of Man? Why not Liverpool? There are over a million and a half children living there.'

I explained how the Isle of Man 'call' had come about and, although we were not sure that he agreed with our proposed move, he did not try to further dissuade us.

The most difficult part was telling our faithful north-west Ulster supporters. The news was greeted mostly with disbelief and with not a few tears.

'But how can you leave such thriving work to go to a small island?'

Anne was reminded of and shared a verse from Psalm 127 (AV):

'Except the Lord build the house they labour in vain that build it.'

And I reminded our teachers of one of the lessons recently taught from Acts, where Phillip is taken from a big ministry in Samaria to witness to one man, an Ethiopian, in the desert.

A former summer missionary, Rhoda Gilfillan, who had been to Bible college and had attended a Kilchzimmer institute, joined us for training. She was a very accomplished and experienced student who had taught in many Good News Clubs and teacher training classes, and whom we knew was more than capable of taking over the north-west area ministry on completion of her training. But that would not be our decision to make.

Chapter Five

In March of 1989 Anne and I were back once more in the Isle of Man, and this time Karen was with us. During this visit we were able to stay at No. 18 Windsor Road and also visit Ballakermeen High School, where we were given a tour by the principal. Karen had with her the syllabus from her present school Foyle College but, as we suspected, the Isle of Man curriculum was different. By this time, though, Karen was reconciled to the thought of having to repeat her year. She was duly registered to start there in September.

During that visit, Paul and Karen Sayers had invited to their home a number of Isle of Man Christians whom they felt we should meet. Among these were some who would become very close and supportive friends: Kevin and Helen Vondy and Helen's parents Ken and Joan Quane (Manx surnames), and Graham and Joan Lewis, and the SU worker Beth Kissick was also there. We outlined our programme for our new ministry and most were quite excited at the prospect of our coming, but Beth wondered if the Island really needed another children's ministry. Before we came to begin our ministry, however, we learned that Beth had become disillusioned, especially with the lack of support regarding her work in primary schools, and had resigned.

Anne and I were also asked to speak to the SNIF group, a strange name for a Baptist youth group, but the initials stood for Saturday Night in Fellowship. A lovely group, some of whom were more spiritual than others, but they were very receptive to Anne sharing on our work and my Bible message. They had learned that during that weekend I was celebrating my 50th birthday, and I received a card from the group which I remember well. The verse read, 'Mirror, Mirror, on the wall, who is the handsomest of all?' After turning the page, it went on to read, 'Cliff Richard, but you are not too far behind!'

We returned after what was a very encouraging and productive long weekend, greatly encouraged further by the feedback that followed.

The following May, Anne and I again attended the European CEF Conference held that year in Germany. There was quite a large group attending, so Anne and I travelled to Belfast where we joined them. A bus was hired to take us to the airport and then off we flew. Our group formed a choir to sing at the conference and I had the privilege of leading the morning prayer meetings. Each morning I shared about the Lord Jesus using the title 'This Man'. No travelling upsets on that occasion.

Over the next few months we had lots of things to organise, and also during this time the committee appointed Rhoda Gilfillan to the north-west Ulster directorship. There were many goodbyes, and a special farewell evening was organised by the committee.

With Rhoda now in charge of the north-west Ulster area, and leaving Richard in our Irish Street home, Anne and I booked our passage to the Isle of Man. Our car packed with as much as we could manage, and with Karen on board, we left north-west Ulster to begin life on the Island.

CHAPTER SIX

Every August in the town of Ramsey in the north of the Island, an outreach to children took place. This outreach was known as the 'tent mission' because, as the name suggests, the meetings were held in a large hired tent. The mission was organised by Bethel Church, the church that Kevin and Helen Vondy attended. Anne and I were approached by Kevin who asked us if we would take over the teaching for the forthcoming programme. We also chatted through the various possibilities for a wider outreach in the north of the Island, and decided it might be a good idea to invite some of the Irish team to come and help. This was organised by our son Richard and Karen Dallas; Karen had helped with the CEF summer clubs in Limavady and Claudy, Co Londonderry. Adrian was part of the team, home after his first year at university. The team arrived early in August and Kevin, Helen, Anne and I met with them in Helen and Kevin's home in Ramsey. The first thing was to sort out accommodation etc. Again hospitality was excellent, and so began our week's programme of teaching, missionary stories and games.

The Ramsey tent mission week concluded with a treasure hunt in the orchard on the farm of John and Aline Cannell. This was followed by a barbecue, and then a parents' evening held in the Cannells' large barn. During this period of outreach Five Day Clubs were held in Andreas in the north, and a few in other parts of the Island.

Another tired but wonderful team returned to Ireland with many memories and stories. They assured us they would return next year if possible. We were also truly thankful for the volunteers from each of the areas who helped that summer. Shortly after this Anne and I received a letter from Richard in which he apologised for being so negative and said that, following his experiences during the week of mission, he was now convinced we were where God wanted us to be.

It was now time for another move, so I hired a van and in late August, leaving Karen with our friends on the Island, we booked with Steam Packet and paid another visit to No. 71 Irish Street. We had tried unsuccessfully to sell our house, and with Richard staying there we could only take so much with us. The important items were our CEF teaching materials. Another van was hired and we loaded up some of our furniture. The local committee chairman, Norman Somerville, drove one van, accompanied by his wife and daughter. I drove the other van, and so Anne and I headed off to begin setting up home in the Isle of Man.

The arrangement with Fiona was that Anne and I could use the downstairs back room as an office, and the living room for social or work-related events. For this, and two bedrooms, we would contribute towards the housekeeping costs and mortgage. I feel I should add at this point that the house had other occupants; Kath and Hilary, who were both teachers, and Joelle who worked in finance. Kath, Hilary and Fiona are still on the Island and continue as 'old' friends. Having deposited our furniture and CEF-related materials at No. 18 Windsor Road, Douglas, we spent the days between boats exploring the Island. Norman and family returned with the van which was signed back into the hire garage.

A generous act worth recording is that because there was a delay in transferring our bank account from Londonderry to the Isle of Man, a friend from Broadway Baptist Church gave us a substantial monetary gift to help out until we had our Isle of Man account opened.

Once settled in to our new abode, Anne, Karen and I soon established a Good News Club in Windsor Road, and a Youth Challenge ministry in Broadway Baptist Church incorporating the former SNIF group; Karen's input to this ministry was invaluable.

Meanwhile, our son Richard, who was now living by himself in the house at No. 71 Irish Street with only our dog Sparky for company, really missed the family. There were, however, two things that helped him to cope. One was his growing relationship with our former volunteer helper Karen Dallas, and the other was Adrian's presence during his work experience from university.

At the invitation of Pastor Gordon, I accompanied the pastor to some of the Douglas area school assemblies which he regularly visited. He introduced me to head teachers in Pulrose, Murray's Road and Anagh Coar schools. Right away I was invited to take morning assemblies in those schools once a month. During the weeks that passed Anne and I travelled throughout the Island, stopping at schools and churches and praying that God would open the doors of His choosing. I then visited all of the Island's schools, speaking with the head teachers and showing the teaching materials I would use in assemblies. Gradually the school ministry grew, with not only monthly assemblies but, for Anne and I, lunchtime clubs opening up as well.

Beth Kissack, the former Scripture Union worker on the Island, had established a number of lunchtime SU clubs in many Island schools. Anne and I took over these clubs with great results, and we added after school clubs to our programme. The clubs eventually became Good News Clubs following the CEF curriculum.

We also met with and encouraged Christians to open their homes for Good News Clubs, and established a weekly teacher training evening in Windsor Road. This was well-attended and so the ministry grew.

During our next summer tent mission, a major problem arose. During the night before the programme was due to commence a strong wind blew up. The centre pole of the tent shattered and the tent collapsed. Not to be outdone Kevin came up with a solution. Some years ago he had helped Val English, who was then an itinerant evangelist, by driving a bus to various areas of the Island, where Val conducted children's meetings. The bus was still in Kevin's garage and was recommissioned as a substitute for the tent. Fortunately, numbers weren't as big that summer, so the bus accommodated the children. We were delighted with the success, but decided that for the following summer we would hire the local infant school.

That summer a young man named Mark Shallcross joined us at the Five Day Club held in Willaston, an area of Douglas, and he became a very enthusiastic helper. I couldn't help noticing as the week went on that he and our daughter Karen became very chatty. This led to Mark and Karen going out together a number of times. Mark loaned me a computer to help with the work, but I must admit to making lots of errors which he had to come and fix. The computer was, however, a great help in putting together a growing school assembly programme.

In the school assemblies I used what were known as flashcards; pictures in a book used to tell a Bible story or a related illustration. One morning, while teaching on the Bible story of the prodigal son, I used an illustration and story of a boy stealing money from his mother's purse in order to buy a 'psychedelic pencil'. After my talk the headmaster, on closing the assembly, said:

'Well, I am so glad Mr Porter spoke today about stealing, because I was shocked to hear earlier this morning that some items have been stolen from a pupil in this school. I hope, like the boy in Mr Porter's story, that someone will come forward and confess.'

Not quite the point I was trying to get across, but a good moral illustration never goes amiss!

I received a phone call one day from a headmistress of an infant school to say that some of the pupils thought I was God, and could I perhaps put this right at the next assembly. So, with the story of one of the miracles of Jesus, who of course I stressed was God in human form, I made it clear that I could not do the miraculous things that God could do. As Anne was standing near the queue of youngsters waiting to leave assembly, she was asked by one boy, 'Where does Mr Porter live?' Only to hear another young boy quickly answer, 'Don't be silly, he lives in heaven!' Oh dear, it seems I didn't manage to make a convincing argument.

Along with an increase in Good News Clubs in homes and schools, the youth ministry also grew under Karen's enthusiastic leadership, but change was in the air. I was invited to speak at the Bayview Brethren service in Port St Mary. The assembly, strengthened by Broadway Baptist members who lived in the south, met for worship service on Sunday morning, with a Gospel service at 4pm. It was at the 4pm service I preached, with Anne in attendance. We were invited to visit Will and Gladys Payne on the following Tuesday morning for tea; Will was an elder in the Bayview assembly. My car was in the garage for a service and some repairs, so Joelle offered her car. It was a dreadful rainy morning and the floor of Joelle's car leaked. After a few wrong turns we finally found Will and Gladys, but by then our shoes and Anne's handbag were soaked. However, we put that behind us and had a very pleasant morning with this lovely elderly and very spiritual couple.

At that time we were regular worshippers in Broadway Baptist, but Will suggested we move south and help in the Port St Mary Fellowship. We explained the circumstances regarding our house in Londonderry, but Will suggested we look at houses in the south anyway. We looked at several houses, but the south was the most expensive place to live being near the airport. We saw some lovely houses but the cheapest was £65,000, and that was for just two bedrooms. Eventually we found a suitable house in Ballasalla, a village about 9km from Port St Mary; if only we could have afforded it. The highest price we were offered for our home in Londonderry was £28,000. After another phone call from Will we visited him and Gladys again. He talked about providing a mortgage for house purchase, but even his generous repayments were too much for us. By now readers will have guessed that Will Payne was a man of means. He then suggested that his trust buy our house in Londonderry to sell on. Having seen pictures of the house Will was convinced it would fetch a good price. Arrangements were made for Anne and me, with Will and Gladys, to fly to Northern Ireland, hire a car and travel to Londonderry to view No. 71 Irish Street.

Chapter Six

The Gideons, a mission dear to Will's heart, was an organisation dedicated to distributing the Scriptures and evangelism. In the Isle of Man, Will often visited churches and schools, speaking about the importance of the Scriptures and giving out New Testaments. We had friends in Londonderry, Alistair and Francis Craig, who had hosted a CEF prayer meeting during our time in north-west Ulster. Alistair and Francis had recently joined the Londonderry branch of the Gideons and were keen to meet with Will; indeed they insisted that Will and Gladys stay overnight with them. Anne and I took Will and Gladys to meet Alistair and Francis before going to view No. 71 Irish Street.

Once he had seen the house Will was keen to meet with a solicitor and finalise the arrangements. Having met our sons Adrian and Richard, Will and Gladys insisted we eat out. We had dinner in the Everglades Hotel where Adrian, bless him, gave a 'Thank You' speech to Will and Gladys. Later we took our guests to Alistair and Francis, and then joined Adrian and Richard to sleep for the last time in our old home. Adrian, by the way, was on a 'sandwich course' at Napier University in Edinburgh. He spent some time at Napier and some in work placement. His work was with my old firm in Maydown, Londonderry, which is why he was staying with Richard.

The following day Anne took Gladys shopping in Londonderry, and Will and I met with a Christian solicitor. Following discussions and advice, it was agreed that Will would buy No. 71 Irish Street for £30,000, plus £3,000 for furnishings. Transaction complete, we flew back to the Isle of Man.

On our return Anne and I contacted John Bingham, a fellow countryman and the manager of an Isle of Man building society. We made an appointment to see him at his office, and there discussed our financial needs. Although I was over 50, John was able to arrange a mortgage suitable for our requirements and with capital repayments. With the purchase of our new home complete we were ready to move again and so, with help from our friends in Broadway Baptist Church, we transferred our furniture and belongings from No. 18 Windsor Road, Douglas to No. 2 Peveril Villas, Ballasalla.

One Sunday morning when Anne and I were worshipping with the church in Port St Mary, we were welcomed by the elder, Will Payne, into fellowship with the Bayview Brethren assembly. Anne and I had now gone from Presbyterian to Baptist to Brethren; we felt truly interdenominational!

On another day Will Payne came to visit and he asked about our financial commitments. He then told us of his plan, with our permission, to set up what he would call 'The Porter Committee'. This was Will's idea to help with the purchase of our house. He drafted a letter 'to whom it may concern', stating that a bank account had been opened in the name of the Porter committee. The committee consisted of Will and Gladys Payne, and Roy and Anne Porter. In the letter Will explained that Anne and I were missionaries, living by faith and working with the Child Evangelism Fellowship reaching out to the children and youth in the Isle of Man. He was seeking help with the purchase of our new home. He then stated that the Payne Trust would put up £7,500, and asked for the recipients of the letter to match this pound for pound. The letter was sent to various churches, Brethren assemblies and individuals throughout the British Isles and beyond. The result was amazing; within days we had over £15,000 in the Porter committee account. Finance continued to come in, and each time the sum reached £1,000 we paid that amount off our mortgage. This greatly reduced the sum owing, enabling us, when the gifts had finished, to pay off the remainder by monthly instalments. In a very short while we were debt-free.

God is so wonderful, and used so many lovely people to assist us, in oh so many ways.

Our son Richard now had employment as a microbiologist in a laboratory in Dundonald, and was preparing to move and live in Belfast. Once again we made a trip to Londonderry to take the rest of our personal belongings, including Sparky our dog, to No. 2 Peveril Villas. This time we were indebted to Mrs Aline Cannell for the use of her van.

Once settled back on the Island, Anne and I sought out some supportive friends who would form a committee, similar to the one we had in north-west Ulster. We invited David and Molly McQuilken, the CEF of Ireland national directors, to visit. Paul and Karen Sayers again played hosts, this time to the prospective committee. At that meeting David shared how important it was for a growing work to have an overseeing committee to whom Anne and I would report. This committee would look after the area finances and help with meetings etc. Those who agreed to become the official Isle of Man CEF committee and take office were Gary Haire, chairman, Paul Sayers, treasurer, Joy Payne, secretary and members Kevin and Helen Vondy, Mona Radcliffe, Keith Allen and Malcolm Kenny.

Prior to David and Molly coming, I had asked David to bring a Bible lesson with him. He accompanied me to the Ballasalla school where he taught at the assembly. He was so pleased to be able to use his skills again. During their visit we took David and Molly on a tour of the Island. Molly remarked how the Island seemed to have four seasons in one day. We stopped in Peel on the west of the Island, and with the weather reasonable we took a walk along the harbour. Everything seemed fine, the sun was shining, and then suddenly a wave swept over the harbour wall and David got most of it. Poor Molly, she was so concerned about him.

We hurried back to the car and got David home as quickly as possible to dry out; there were no ill effects.

A short time later we introduced the CEF correspondence course to the committee, which Helen Vondy agreed to conduct. This proved once again to be a very successful way of reaching children with the Scriptures.

Over the years the assembly in Port St Mary had diminished in numbers. Members had grown old or passed away, but because a number of Broadway Baptist members attended the services, the evangelical Christian witness in Port St Mary was maintained. Negotiations, however, were underway for the fellowship in Port St Mary to become a sister church to Broadway Baptist. After much discussion the agreed sister church was established, and named Port St Mary Baptist Church. The eldership comprised me, Will Payne and Robin Oake, who at that time was the Isle of Man chief constable. Over the next few years the church membership grew, and I had the privilege of sharing the preaching and conducting many baptisms. Anne and I helped with the Sunday school and established a midweek Good News Club in the church hall. Soon a PA system was installed and Sunday messages recorded. Anne and Chris Oake, Robin's wife, were also the church cleaners, meeting along with others each Saturday morning to sweep and polish.

Anne and I had brought with us from Ireland a Vauxhall Cavalier. The car, which replaced the one we had in Switzerland, had served us well during our time in north-west Ulster, but I was finding a car with no power steering to be a tough drive on the Isle of Man roads. Then an overhaul of the engine was required, and it was also not cost efficient as petrol consumption was increasing.

One day a lady friend from church called and asked if there something wrong with my car. I told her about some of the problems I was having, and asked her why she was asking.

Chapter Six

'Well,' she replied, 'in church on Sunday I felt, no, heard, God speaking to me. He told me to give my car to the Porters, so here I am. If you run me home my car is yours to do with as you please.'

As Anne and I followed her to the car park we tried to remember what kind of car she drove; we seemed to remember a small red one. To say we were 'gobsmacked' would be putting it mildly when we stopped beside a silver-grey Toyota Corolla Executive with just 728 miles on the clock; I think I cried! I drove our friend home in her, now our, car, with Anne in the passenger seat. Words could not express our gratitude for such an amazing gift. This wonderful car was such a joy to drive, and drive I did, all over the Island. Anne and I calculated that during our time working in the Isle of Man we covered around 2,000 miles each month visiting assemblies, Good News Clubs and church meetings etc., in an Island roughly 33 miles long by 13 miles wide.

David Lewis, a young man who helped in our summer outreach and who lived just around the corner from us in Ballasalla, helped me to convert half the garage into an office. I remember that time very well because David and I, ardent Arsenal supporters, listened in horror to the radio commentary on a match whereby a lower league team, Wrexham, played and beat Arsenal in the fourth round of the FA Cup - disaster! But the office turned out rather well. I had purchased a word processor with only 120 characters but I found this a tremendous advantage over my wee blue typewriter. It was very useful, though slow, however, when I discovered that the Irish CEF Constitution and Trust Deed were not acceptable in the Isle of man. So, prayerfully, painstakingly and with advice from David McQuilken, I constructed a new CEF Isle of Man Constitution and Trust Deed. Then Anne and I needed trustees, so we prayed and contacted various friends. Each one we contacted was willing to become a trustee, so I submitted the paperwork to the relevant government department and it was accepted. With prayers of thankfulness Anne and I came before the Lord that day.

On one occasion I was taking two young Youth Challenge members home to St Johns when I overheard a strange conversation:

No. 1: 'What have you got?'

No. 2: 'I've got a 486xs.'

No. 1: 'Has it got windows?'

No. 2: 'Of course!'

The conversation ended there because we had reached our destination, but once back home I was on the phone to Paul Sayers.

'Paul, what is a 486xs?'

'It's a computer, the latest model.'

'And why does it have windows?'

'Oh, that's the name of the operating system.'

'Paul, I need one.'

The committee granted my request, and I became the proud owner of the latest model 486xs desktop computer with Windows plus a printer. The gentleman who delivered it and set it up spent an hour with me, instructing me on the basics and taking me through the tutorial. Over the next months this tutorial became my best friend.

Adrian visited us each summer and he, Karen, Anne and I took our Senior Youth Challenge group for a weekend of Bible teaching and training for outreach. This was held in Eary Cushlin, a former farmhouse now used as a youth centre. Karen, Adrian and I conducted the weekend activities; Anne was our house mother and cook, with help from friends. As a family we also led teams teaching Five Day Clubs and Holiday Bible Clubs each summer.

CHAPTER SEVEN

'I don't know about you, but I love pigs.' This was usually my opening phrase when teaching the Bible lesson on the prodigal son. When the young people involved with us met for fun evenings, this opening, along with my accompanying actions, was a young man David's party piece. It is said that one of the greatest compliments that can be paid is imitation. Well, I hope so.

I previously wrote about some of the youth from north-west Ulster who were now in full or part-time ministry. This is also true of some of the Isle of Man youth who worked with Anne and me. The previously mentioned David became a church pastor, James a curate, Kristina spent time working with a mission in Africa and others became involved in their churches. Blessed memories of wonderful young folk still being mightily used by God.

Our daughter Karen had decided on physiotherapy as a career. While looking at universities and colleges she was invited to visit a teaching hospital in Manchester. In late summer I booked a sailing to Liverpool and Anne, Karen and I motored to Manchester. We had arranged to stay the night with a former CEF worker now pastoring a church there. Next day Anne, Karen and I visited the Manchester hospital, parked in the car park, and I walked Karen to her interview room. We planned to meet afterwards in the car park. As time went by Anne and I grew concerned about her, and I walked into the hospital to search for her without success. I came back to see if she had arrived at the car park, and there found a tearful Karen who explained that she had gone to the wrong exit and got lost. We left hospital and then began an exasperating search for the main road to Liverpool. We seemed to be constantly confronted by roadworks and diversions. Very frustrated, we eventually found our way out and had a speedy journey to catch the late boat to the Isle of Man. As far as Karen was concerned, Manchester was a no-go with regards to her future.

I mention this episode because a few weeks later I received a phone call from the CEF European director, Sam Doherty. He asked me to cancel the next day's agenda because he was coming to visit and wanted to spend the day with us. On arrival and after a cup of tea, Sam talked about being impressed with our ministry and suggested that we could perhaps expand it. CEF of Great Britain was seeking national directors and he felt that Anne and I would have the ability to fill that position. Sam's idea was that by taking on this role we could incorporate the work in the Isle of Man, the Island, after all, being a part of Great Britain. We would, however, have to leave the Island and work from the head office in… Manchester (Karen's response when we told her? 'Well, you don't think I'm coming to visit if you move there!').

Anne and I had, each Thursday, prayed exclusively for CEF Great Britain, and as we said goodbye to Sam we said that this was something we would have to seriously pray about. As an essential part of our ministry, Anne and I had established prayer meetings in homes in the Douglas, Ramsey, Port Erin and Peel areas. There was a lot of negativity in those meetings, and in the committee meeting, when we shared Sam's proposition. Although Anne and I did pray a lot about the proposed move we had no peace about it. Our feelings were that if this was God's will and we turned it down then the ministry in the Isle of Man would diminish. Whatever the rights and wrongs of such thinking, we did turn down the proposition and, during the months that followed, the CEF ministry in the Isle of Man went from strength to strength.

On completing his time at university Adrian tried, unsuccessfully, to find suitable employment in Northern Ireland. I suggested he come and live for a year in the Isle of Man, which he did. There he had no problem finding part-time work as a gardener, carpet-fitter and sheep-herder. Adrian's own story would fill a book by itself so I will just give a brief summary: along with his sister Karen he was part of the music scene in Port St Mary Baptist Church, he helped the Stauros worker Dewi Humphries at his drop-in, he tried his hand (unsuccessfully) at stock-car racing, he married his sweetheart Madeleine Stewart, and he was employed firstly making test equipment for a kettle manufacturer, before being taken on as part of the engineering staff within that company. He and Madeleine bought a house in Ballasalla; Madeleine, as a nurse, soon found employment at the hospital in Douglas.

Anne and I were now travelling all over the Island conducting school assemblies, lunchtime clubs and evening Good News Clubs. We also had a weekly youth meeting in our home in Ballasalla. To help with this I had permission, after doing a test, to use the Education Authority minibus. I also had the use of a minibus loaned to us, when needed, by the Vondy garage in Andreas. These came in very handy for our adventure and teaching weekends for Junior and Senior

Youth Challenge groups. On those weekends Adrian, Madeleine and Karen (when available) were a great help. The committee also purchased an old yellow minibus which was in reasonable condition, so transport of our young people was now no problem. One of the many highlights of the youth ministry were the weekend activities held in a camp centre in Maughold, outside the town of Ramsey. I say a camp centre, but it was a converted stable yard with only adequate facilities. The dorms where we slept had three-tier bunk beds constructed from tree branches, with strong plastic tarpaulin as hammocks, and toilets were outside. Today's health and safety organisations would never have approved, but we had some good laughs about sleeping, or lack of it, and no one came to any harm. On one such weekend Anne and I took the seats out of the minibus and slept there. Anne had filled our hot water bottle for one of the group, and at about two in the morning there was a knock on the door of the minibus. The young camper standing there held out the hot water bottle and said, 'Here, I don't need this anymore.'

Bible teaching and worship, go-karting, archery, an assault course (for the more energetic) at the neighbouring venture centre, barbecues and chorus-singing around a campfire are just some of the many wonderful memories of our youth weekends at the camp centre. Adrian and Madeleine eventually took over the Youth Challenge ministry and also shared many exciting moments and memories.

Karen was at university but still came home and organised the summer programmes. Anne and I, however, never felt obsolete. Team members now came not just from Ireland, but also from Scotland and England. We and our ministry were richly blessed.

Gary Haire, who had then handed over the local committee chair to Kevin Vondy, also reviewed song and music tapes for a

UK-based Christian publisher. He passed some of these tapes on to Anne and me to listen to while motoring. Things were not going well with me health-wise; arthritis was causing me lots of left hand and arm pain. Guitar playing was becoming difficult, as was driving. Travelling to take an assembly one morning, I was listening to a tape of an American Christian artist, Don Meon, singing a song based on Exodus 15:26 (AV), 'I am the God that healeth thee.' Don then spoke and said:

'Do you believe this?'

As I travelled I prayed, with my eyes open of course.

'Yes Lord, I believe, help my unbelief.'

The sensation that travelled through my body was indescribable, and right there and then the pain in my left hand and arm was gone. Now in my older years, I still have problems with arthritis, but I have never again experienced the arthritic pain I had during that period in the Isle of Man. Without that healing, my ministry would have suffered and what followed would have been extremely difficult.

After a morning service in Port St Mary Baptist Church at which David Gordon preached, we had a barbecue in the garden of two members, Mike and Mary Darnill. During a conversation with David, he told Anne and I about an idea he had for an extension to the church in Broadway. Next door to the church two guest houses had come on the market for sale. One was a large double-fronted house, the other a single. As they were in very poor condition the price was very tempting. David thought that if he could persuade Broadway Church to buy both properties, then perhaps other organisations such as CEF would take on the task of renovating a floor of one of the guest houses for use in their ministry. Anne and I met with David to look at the buildings. David told us that a member of the church was prepared to buy the smaller of the two properties, leaving the church with just the larger house to renovate. As we looked around we could see the immensity of the work, plus the finance that would be required. Prayer, prayer and more prayer would be fervently needed, so Anne and I shared the project with our prayer partners. Broadway Church purchased the properties and sold one to their church member.

Thus the Alpha Centre was born, but the renovation work required was daunting. The church folk, under David's organisation, worked on the top floors and bookshop. Dewi Humphries, with help, undertook part of the second floor to create a Stauros drop-in centre, and the CEF committee took on the task of renovating the basement. Here I want to mention some of the amazing people with whom Anne and I created what came to be known as AlphaBase:

Derek Hayes, Malcolm Newton, Mike Justice, Malcolm Kenny, Adrian Porter, Paul Sayers, Keith Allen, and Robert Webb, a plumber who gave his time free and installed the central heating for just the cost of materials. There are others whose names I am afraid I have forgotten, but who came each Saturday morning and not a few evenings to clear out rubble, level new cement floors, build toilets and a kitchen and clean and decorate.

Planning permission was needed to allow new street-level double-glazed doors and windows to be installed. Anne had outlined her ideas and presented her floor plan to our architect Nigel Chaplin. With very few changes Nigel drew up the plans and presented them to the planning department; planning went through quickly and with no adjustments. Anne and I look back with some amusement at our involvement. I went each morning to an assembly, and then picked up Anne for work in the basement. Next we had a quick wash and lunch before setting off for a lunchtime club, and then we returned to the basement. Firstly it was rubble-gathering, and later, when ceiling and walls were plastered, painting, then tea and our evening programmes. We left the professional work to professionals, but the work of the volunteers saved CEF a lot of money. Carpets and curtains were gifts from friends, and Anne had a ball with decorating the kitchen and doing some of the wallpapering. The basement was divided into two rooms which were separated by a partition wall and portable sound panels, so we were able to use both rooms at the same time. I believe we renovated and launched the AlphaBase for a little over £18,000. The plan then was that CEF would pay Broadway a peppercorn rent over a five-year period of lease.

The AlphaBase was used for teacher training each Monday evening, and Anne and I held a weekly Good News Club on Tuesdays. Friday evening was our drop-in for young teens; with this we had help from Malcolm Kenny. The kids sat on bean bags which Anne bought. We were also gifted with games equipment. The school in Port St Mary gave a table tennis table, and from the Douglas Head Hotel we received a pool table and chairs, some of which needed repair but they were useful. A television, video player and games console were given along with games, and there were various board games as well. At an auction Anne put in a bid for a collection of cutlery and plates. Her bid was successful and the kitchen was furnished. When collecting an order from the local transport company, I was told about an order of plastic chairs that had not been collected and was apparently unwanted, which was taking up much-needed space. I was asked to cover the storage and administration costs, and for that I could have the chairs. I couldn't pass this up so AlphaBase had seating for over 60 people. From another hotel which was shutting down we purchased very reasonably some small tables and stools. Anne was in charge of the tuck shop and kept prices as low as possible, and she also had control of the kitchen. We held weekly prayer meetings, and Youth Challenge met each Saturday evening. We also held promotional evenings, with food of course, twice yearly.

Each summer Scripture Union held a beach mission in Port St Mary based at a property named Dublin House. Over the years, with the increase in children attending, more leaders were needed and larger accommodation was required. As part of the CEF ministry, 'thank you' evenings were held each March using the British Red Cross facility in Douglas. These evenings took the form of a meal, reports and a final challenge from a guest speaker. The purpose of the meetings was, as the name suggests, to thank all who had helped and supported the work during the previous year. The assistant European director, Roy Harrison, was our guest speaker during the time when Dublin House was under discussion about its future. With permission Anne and I took Roy to see the house and the area. He was convinced that Dublin House would make an excellent CEF camp house, and asked us to make enquiries should the house become available. It was brought to our attention that the two houses adjacent to Dublin House were on the market for sale. The larger of the two was named Malmore, and in our church on Sunday morning Mrs Alexander, a lady who was associated with the charitable trust which owned Dublin House, was present. After the service I approached her and told her of the availability of Malmore, but her reply was rather scathing and so I left it at that.

During the next week Anne and I learned that a Christian entrepreneur, Mr Graham Lacey, was interested in purchasing Malmore and the adjoining smaller property. I also learned that Mr Lacey had purchased and was living in and working from the former bishop's residence, Bishopscourt, in Kirk Michael. Taking, as it were, my cap in my hand, I called at Bishopscourt and saw not Mr Lacey but his personal assistant.

I explained to her our interest in property in Port St Mary, and said that I wondered if, should Mr Lacey buy Malmore, he would sell it on to CEF. I left my name and telephone number, and a few days later Mr Lacey rang me. He suggested that he would continue with the purchase and then we could discuss the sale of Malmore to CEF. Anne and I, with some members of the committee, contacted the gentleman who was still occupying the smaller property, and he showed us around both houses. We were quite excited about the larger house, and once again I contacted Mr Lacey. I told him that the two properties were interconnected; walls had been opened up and doors installed to allow movement between both houses. When Mr Lacey's solicitor heard this he did not encourage the transaction, so Mr Lacey decided that he would back down, but that he would ask the estate agent in charge to sell to us for the amount he had bid, which was well below the asking price. The estate agent called me and said that he didn't understand what was going on, but he would put the bid again to the owners. The bid was accepted and so CEF Isle of Man with, hopefully, help from Europe and Ireland, began looking at ways of raising the finances. A considerable sum of money was placed at our disposal so we went forward encouraged. Shortly after this I received a phone call from Mrs Alexander proposing that she and the trust she represented join with CEF in the purchase of Malmore. After much discussion, Anne and I and the CEF committee had no peace about the proposed alliance. So, and with a whole lot of prayer, it was decided that Mrs Alexander and her trustees, if willing, should take over the project, which they agreed to do. I honestly felt quite thankful because the whole business was having a detrimental effect on Anne's health. We were now convinced that a CEF camp house in the Isle of Man was perhaps not part of God's plan.

CHAPTER EIGHT

Preparation was made as usual for the summer programme although, by this time, our Holiday Bible Club in Douglas was run as a day camp with a full day's programme. The morning programme was the usual Holiday Bible Club incorporating all age groups. The team would break for lunch, then meet with the 10 to 12-year-olds for games or outings. One afternoon during the week was always assigned to 'hunt the worker'. As outlined previously, this involved the leaders dressing up as workers, and placing themselves in various locations which the 'campers' had to find. They would then challenge the 'worker' with a prearranged question which only a genuine leader would know. Once again there was some fun and embarrassment when an approach was made to someone who turned out to be a complete stranger. I remember some Japanese visitors to Port Erin taking pictures with amusement of a chimney sweep (Malcolm Newton) carrying his brushes as he walked along the Port Erin beach. That was just one of the many costumes used by leaders during our 'hunt the worker' activities. Adrian, Karen and Malcolm Kenny looked after the evening activities with the older age group.

Chapter Eight

During the morning session at the Douglas Holiday Bible Club when Anne had finished telling the missionary story, I noticed that she was sitting down and her face was quite pale. I asked Kevin Vondy, who was helping, to take charge along with Karen and Adrian. I took Anne home and for her, the summer work was over. She rested during the remainder of that and the following week, so, leaving the summer team in charge, I took her for a holiday to Wales. It was a nonevent; she couldn't eat or sleep so I cut the time short and took her home. This was the start of a gradual physical and emotional decline for Anne. I thank God for the help we received from Adrian and Madeleine, and for the home visits of Anne's doctor who made herself available day and night. She thought it would take up to a year for Anne to fully recover, but God responded to the many prayers of our friends and, by the beginning of September, Anne was well on the road to recovery. By October she was again joining me in some school assemblies and lunchtime clubs. Anne and I, however, began to take stock of our workload. When we looked at our programme of activities, we discovered that we were doing over 80 meetings per month, and that did not include those taken by volunteers.

Once more Anne had health problems. This time an X-ray showed that she had a hiatus hernia and the hiatus was quite large. An operation was discussed but that would mean Anne going to Liverpool, a move she was not keen on. She and I were both now finding the workload a bit too much to handle and decided to reduce our commitment. This was not an easy job, as deciding what to do and what not to do proved to be very difficult, and Anne, in spite of her health problems, was worse than me in deciding. We talked with Henry Berry, now the national director of CEF of Ireland, regarding possible replacements. Nothing and no one was forthcoming so I took an executive decision. Without consulting Anne, I wrote a letter of resignation which, at the next committee meeting, I presented to the chairman. The committee members and Anne were stunned, but as the letter explained I felt our stepping down would open the door for our replacements. I was vindicated, because within two months of our (yes, by now Anne was in agreement) decision a couple from Northern Ireland, Geoffrey and Lily Weir, applied to come to the Isle of Man. They came in May of the following year; Geoffrey and I visited the schools I had connections with and soon he was making out his own programme.

The leadership in our church in Port St Mary suggested I take on the pastorate of the church, but this was not to be. However, I still continued to preach on some Sundays and baptise. I also conducted midweek meetings and, with Anne, nurture groups.

Following one of the morning services at which I preached, Mr Graham Lacey, now attending our church, approached me with a proposition. He was holding Saturday evening meetings in Bishopscourt, a few of which Anne and I had attended. He felt that this ministry could be expanded and that I was the person to do this. He invited Anne and I to visit Bishopscourt that week. We called and met with Graham and his lovely wife, Susan, and had a tour of Bishopscourt including the chapel, the organ of which was being overhauled. We chatted about what my role might be in Graham's plan, and he said that the area needed a centre for interdenominational worship and he felt that I could lead this ministry at Bishopscourt. Anne and I prayed about this, and felt that it might be a less exhausting way for Anne and me to continue serving God in a new area. Discussions with Graham followed. He said that he would contribute to the support of the ministry for a three-year period, and I would continue with weekly Saturday evening meetings with perhaps a monthly Sunday morning family service. Again after a lot of prayer, I, with Anne's backing, agreed.

We both felt, however, that to minister in the area surrounding Kirk Michael we would really need to live there. So, and again with prayer, we drove around the area looking at several houses provided by an estate agent. We let our church know what we were planning and our pianist, Richard Torpy, approached us regarding the purchase of our Ballasalla home. We agreed a price and the plans were set in motion. Mr Lacey owned a property in Kirk Michael which included a flat above an empty shop. This was put at our disposal until such time as a suitable house became available. Our furniture was divided between storage at the rear of the empty shop and a very dry barn at the farm of our dear friends, John and Aline Cannell. We made the flat very homely with new carpet throughout and, purchased from a second-hand shop, a set of wall cabinets which added to the kitchen furnishings. So this was our home for the first six months of our Bishopscourt ministry. We also had a bird's-eye view of the motorbikes racing in the TT and Grand Prix races, as Kirk Michael was part of the course.

Meanwhile we continued looking for a suitable home in Kirk Michael. The homes in a street named The Meadows had a rear outlook towards the sea, and it was while parked in a street looking to the back of The Meadows that we saw our home, or at least the large conservatory. We drove round and looked at what seemed to be an empty property. On our next visit to the estate agent, we mentioned No. 9 The Meadows, and to our surprise he said it was 'sort of' available. The elderly lady who owned the house had taken ill and was in a nursing home, and her daughter, who lived in England, wanted to rent the house; the estate agent, however, was keen to sell. He met with us to look around the property and what we saw, we loved; we intimated that we would be keen to buy. Now I come to another miraculous intervention. The estate agent told the owner's daughter who we were and what we did, and that we would like to buy the house at a certain price. She responded without ever having met us, by telling the estate agent that she would sell the house, but only to the Porters! So we bought the house. Later, after moving in, we received a lovely letter from her wishing us every blessing for the future, and hoping we would enjoy the wonderful sunsets; they were indeed wonderful.

Over the next two years the services in Bishopscourt continued on Saturday evenings, together with monthly family services, and very special Christmas services held the week before Christmas Day. Anne and I also hosted special occasions with guest singers including Whitney Phipps and Graham Kendrick and The Ramsey Choral Society. I still continued to visit the northern schools for assemblies, and Anne and I held a Good News Club in the hall at the chapel in Bishopscourt.

One day the mother of two of the Good News Club children contacted me. She told me that her father was dying, and asked if Anne and I would come and visit and pray with him. She also told us that the rest of the family were Jehovah's Witnesses and she wasn't sure what kind of reception we would receive. Anne and I knew this lady and her husband very well, indeed her husband had helped in the Douglas Holiday Bible Club. We agreed to visit. On the evening of the visit our friend met us and took us into the room where her father lay. Her sister was also present and I could sense her resentment. As I opened my Bible to read, the sister turned the light off saying that it was too bright for her father's eyes. At that moment I thanked God for the privilege of teaching and memorising Scripture. The portion that I was going to read was John 14:1-6, which Anne and I had taught in Good News Clubs the previous year. So from memory I recited the verses:

'Let not your heart be troubled; you believe in God, believe also in me. In my Father's house are many mansions; if it were not so, I would have told you. I go to prepare a place for you.'

I then skipped to the wonderful verse 6 where Jesus said:

'I am the way, the truth, and the life. No one comes to the Father except through me.'

I then prayed with him and we left. She didn't need to say, but I knew that all the time we were there Anne had been praying for me.

We learned later from the Christian daughter that her father didn't die, but had a period of remission. He told her that he had felt God speaking to him, and that he had asked Christ, as he put it, to take charge of his life. She also told us that before he eventually succumbed to his illness he had testified to everyone who came to visit about his wonderful relationship with Jesus. Isn't our God an amazing God?

On another evening a lady arrived late for the service. She sat at the back and left before the closing hymn. We discovered later that she was the mother of one of our dear friends, who lived near the village of Sulby. His son had been a very enthusiastic member of our Sulby school lunchtime club who was always inventing ways of enthusing the other children. When our friend's mother was seriously ill and in hospital, his son was standing by her bedside looking very sad. She took his hand and told him not to worry, she knew she was dying but she had made her peace with God. Anne and I don't know whether or not this had happened following her visit to Bishopscourt, but we discovered later that our friend had constantly prayed for his mother because she had shown no interest in things spiritual. Indeed, he had only found out after his mother's death about her one and only visit to Bishopscourt, when his son had told him of his conversation with his gran.

There were many other wonderful moments in our ministry for which Anne and I give God all the Praise and all the Glory.

At Easter we held an Easter egg hunt in the grounds of Bishopscourt, always ending with an Easter message for children and parents. During this time, we were joined by Graham and Joan Lewis who had moved from Douglas to Kirk Michael. Their help was much appreciated, especially in outreach around the area. At one time we visited nearly every house in Kirk Michael asking the householder to accept and view the Jesus video which was very popular at that time. We would return the following week and talk to those who had accepted the video, asking what they thought about the Jesus person and His story. Some very worthwhile contacts were made, and some great discussions took place during those weeks of outreach. With the help of the Lewises, and another friend, Ken Quane, who played accordion, we established a 'Bright Hour' for senior citizens in Kirk Michael, Ballaugh and Sulby. Tea, buns, scones and lots of singing plus a Bible message comprised our programme, and it was well-received. A telephone prayer line was installed in the Bishopscourt library, and prayer requests were received and answered. I held consultations and personally prayed with others who came to the library. Tuesday evening Bible studies took place in our home, in which we studied themes such as 'Intimacy with God', 'Know Why You Believe', 'Giving Away Your Faith' and 'Why Would a Good God Allow Suffering?' I also had the privilege on Friday mornings of meeting with a young Alex Brown, the new SU worker. He and I studied Bible verses, chatted over his work programme and prayed together. During this Friday time Anne and Susan Lacey met in our home for Bible study and prayer.

The Saturday evening meetings continued and were well-attended. A friend from Bethel Church in Ramsey played the newly-restored organ, and a PA system was installed plus screen and overhead projector. Services were recorded, and with this we had the help of our very good friends Roy and Di Killey. Di played banjo and Roy played the harmonica, so Anne and I made sure that on some occasions their talents were used in our services. Anne and I also held an 'After Eight' meeting on Sunday evenings, and with this we were grateful for the help of Adrian, Richard Torpy and friends from other churches in the area. Souls were saved and hurts, both physical and emotional, were healed.

I record these events not to exalt those of us involved in the ministry, but to demonstrate to my readers just how awesome, amazing and wonderful is the God we serve, and I do give God all the Glory.

Although in the Bishopscourt chapel we had some very special Sunday morning services, somehow the establishing of an ongoing Sunday morning ministry was not to be. But again, as I will later record, God knew the big picture.

Our daughter Karen, now studying physiotherapy at St Margaret's College in Edinburgh, was also greatly used for her musical ability; it was through music that she met Euan MacRae. At that time Anne and I had set up a trust to govern the work outside of Bishopscourt, named The Salem Trust. The trustees were Aline Cannell, Chris Oake, Ken Quane and John Gooding, who was our link with Bishopscourt. The 'Salt And Light Evangelical Ministries Trust' met each month to pray for and set up a programme of events.

Our first endeavour was an Easter conference and for this we asked Pastor Val English, who was well-known on the

Island having previously ministered there, to speak. We also asked Karen and Euan to bring over a group of musicians to play at the conference. With hindsight Easter was not the best time for a conference, as people would leave the Island to visit families living elsewhere. Although numbers were not as great as we had hoped, it was, nevertheless, a very enjoyable conference. The programme consisted of a Friday 'Praise Evening' in Port St Mary Baptist Church, led by Karen, Euan and the musicians and at which Val shared the first of his Bible messages. On Saturday morning Val gave his second message but, this time, in the Kirk Michael Methodist Church – kindly granted. There were seminars on worship, children in church and seeker-friendly church services, which were taken by me, Val and Karen. The conference ended with a Saturday evening meeting, including music from the group and a closing message from Val.

It was during that weekend that Euan came to me in the kitchen in Kirk Michael and asked if he could have Karen's hand in marriage. I was delighted to say yes, and couldn't wait to share the news with Anne. Later that year Anne and I travelled to Scotland to attend the engagement of Karen and Euan. We stayed with Euan's mum and dad, Margot and Hamish. We had a lovely time celebrating the engagement, but later that evening there was a phone call from Richard's wife, Karen, to say that Richard had suffered a stroke while playing football. Quickly we packed our bags and left Scotland for Liverpool. From there we took a ferry to the Isle of Man, and then took another ferry to Dublin. We motored up to visit Richard in hospital to find, thankfully, that he was already improving, but it would take a long time to full recovery.

Anne had planned to visit Australia with her sister, Pearl. Their sister Jean lived in Perth, and they had been looking forward to this trip for months. It took some persuading to convince Anne to go, but go she did. I kept her up-to-date with Richard's condition, where all signs of improvement were good.

Having previously visited 'The Nunnery' with Mr Lacey, which was another of his properties, Mr Lacey discussed the possible use of this building and its private chapel. He also suggested that we invite a prominent evangelical and friend from the past, Michael Perrot, with his very accomplished wife, to come over from Ireland and conduct a series of meetings. The first of the meetings was held on a Friday in the British Red Cross Hall in Douglas. That evening, Michael and Mrs Perrot shared some useful help and advice with those who attended; Michael was at that time very much involved in Christian counselling.

The next part of the weekend programme took place in The Nunnery. I would add here that these arrangements had been made prior to Anne's visit to Australia, and it was only the day before the arranged meetings that Anne arrived back from Australia. The Nunnery programme included a men's breakfast and ladies' lunch, and, for Anne, there was no time for jet lag; she was immediately back in ministry mode, although this time as one of the waitresses. Michael spoke at the breakfast, and the speaker at the ladies' lunch was Mrs Perrot. Both were well-attended and very worthwhile. Once again the help of many friends, especially our cook, Derek Hayes, was appreciated.

Our three-year period with Mr Lacey was now almost complete, and having learned that The Nunnery was sold Anne and I felt (or was it God telling us?) that it was time to pray and think about the future of our ministry. We decided to send out a letter to our prayer partners in which we asked for prayer for God's guidance as to the way forward. As it turned out 'The Way Forward' was the title of the last sermon I preached in Bishopscourt.

Henry Berry, the CEF of Ireland national director, was on the Island for the annual CEF fellowship meal at which he was the speaker. Having read our prayer letter, Henry called to see us. He asked if I would consider coming back into CEF as a fieldworker for southern Europe. I was quite excited about this, but Anne was not convinced. So, once again after prayer, and considering Anne's health, I declined. A week later I received two phone calls. The first was from the chairman of the Christian drop-in centre in Limavady, asking Anne and me to take on the role of spiritual supervisors at the drop-in. The second was a call to return to north-west Ulster where the work of CEF was not going well. Rhoda Gilfillan had not stayed long in the work there, as she always felt her calling was to Great Britain and had gone to work with CEF in Manchester. Hugh Moon, the incumbent director, was leaving to take up a post at the National Office, and the committee felt that Anne and I were the couple to help revive the work in the north-west area. Anne and I committed all of this to God in prayer, and our family and others prayed with us. It wasn't too long before God began to show us that His plan was for us to return to CEF in north-west Ulster.

CHAPTER NINE

With our decision made we prepared to resign from the Bishopscourt ministry, so a letter of resignation was given to Mr Lacey. Our next task was to talk with the trustees regarding our proposed return to Ireland and the consequent closing of the Salem Trust. As arranged in the trust, any monies left in the account would be transferred to the work of CEF on the Island.

The house in Kirk Michael was advertised and sold very quickly, and for a good price. But where should we live in Northern Ireland? We both remembered how we had enjoyed several years of camp ministry in Castlerock, a seaside town on the north coast, and so we felt very much inclined to live there. Anne and I booked a sailing to Ireland and, on arrival, called with Karen and Richard. Next day we drove to visit Anne's sister, Pearl, in Portrush. Together we viewed several bungalows in Castlerock, and were very interested in one in Liffock Park. Anne and I made an appointment to view, and discussed a price. The owner said, 'No, too low, I want my asking price.' Anne and I then visited an estate agent who was selling new builds in the same place. We viewed the only one available, but it was not what we wanted, so Anne said, 'Let's go back to the other bungalow and up our offer.'

As we approached the front door the lady of the house opened it.

'I'm so glad you have come back. We have decided, if it is still there, to accept your offer,' she said.

We agreed a price including curtains, carpets and fittings and went off to find a solicitor. Within a few weeks we were packing up in Kirk Michael and again sailing for Ireland. When everything had been completed, we set about applying to once again become part of the CEF of Ireland. Not long after our move we learned that Bishopscourt had been sold.

It was strange, more for the National Committee than for us, to be interviewed. All went through smoothly, and Anne and I were back in our beloved children's ministry and in our home territory. To reintroduce ourselves to the friends of CEF in the north-west area, we travelled to some of the districts showing on PowerPoint a presentation that we named 'Reflections'. Using this we reminded folks of our past ministry, showing some of them in action in various CEF clubs. This, of course, was accompanied by refreshments and plenty of chat. God began to move in a marvellous way, and the north-west CEF ministry was soon growing, practically and financially, once again. However, with our increasing years Anne and I both felt that our role was short-term, and we urged the committee to pray regarding future replacements.

We joined Portstewart Baptist Church, where our friend Val English was pastor, and enjoyed the fellowship and teaching there. I also had opportunities to preach in church and speak to the children. During the summer, because of the numbers attending, Anne and I were asked to take on a 'Children's Church' during the morning services. This we enjoyed very much, but although we had help we found it very exhausting, so we mostly hosted Sunday lunch at the Lodge Hotel carvery in Coleraine. I was asked to speak at the closing meeting of one of the church's SU summer programmes, and at New Horizon (an annual Bible Week held at the university in Coleraine) I was invited to conduct one of the children's morning meetings.

Meanwhile we were still enjoying the growing CEF ministry in north-west Ulster, especially in the schools. I was well-received but I think I came second to 'Henry'; this was the name I had christened my Yamaha guitar. You will recall the tragic story of the guitar's accident when its neck was broken and repaired, and consequently it could only have six strings as opposed to the original twelve. The story of poor Henry was received very sympathetically by the assembly pupils, especially the younger ones.

The school assembly programme was expanding and well-received. Many of the older primary pupils now made up a big number of the summer camp attendees. They also attended many of the Holiday Bible Clubs, so numbers there increased. Because of this more volunteers were needed to get involved in the area. So prayer and gentle persuasion were required; soon the number of volunteers increased!

The summer camp was now meeting in Ballycastle Primary School. Ballycastle was another lovely coastal town with a good beach and, for the children's activities, it was a safe town. The 'hunt the worker' was again a big highlight of the week, and shoppers in Ballycastle were amazed to see two large 'teletubbies' parading around the streets. The following year Ballycastle School was unavailable, so we returned to our old venue, Castlerock's Hezlett Primary School. We were not to know, however, that God was seeing the big picture, and events were about to happen which would result in more change, more quickly than we could have imagined.

To celebrate our 40th wedding anniversary, the family decided that Anne and I should take a holiday. After a family dinner at a hotel in Ballymena, and an evening at the Opera House in Belfast to see 'Hello Dolly', we headed off to Cyprus. The hotel was lovely, the weather marvellous, the food and entertainment were excellent, and the pool was both relaxing and exhilarating. Then, on our second morning there, it happened.

After swimming in the pool Anne videoed me in the Jacuzzi, then we relaxed on our sunbeds. Suddenly my world was changing. Something not right was happening. I could feel a strange sensation of everything closing in on me. I told Anne, who thought it might be something to do with the sun, but I knew differently. I went to the pool bar and asked that the hotel doctor be informed. As I sat on a chair a lady, who was also on holiday and was from Belfast, looked at me and told Anne, 'I know by his colour that your husband is having a heart attack.' The hotel doctor arrived and immediately called for an ambulance. In a very short time it arrived, and so did the pain. I have never before or since suffered such excruciation. I remember praying, not to live, but for the pain to go away. I knew very little else about the next two days, but found myself in a private clinic attended by three doctors, and on medication which the clinic doctor informed Anne that Tony Blair would not pay for! Anne handled the situation very well with help from the lovely lady from Belfast. The clinic put Anne in a bed beside me, and in many ways she was my nurse. Richard came out on Monday, the earliest flight he could find, and I was in the clinic for the remainder of our holiday period. So after our 40th anniversary stay in Cyprus, we returned home to be met by ambulance in Belfast and whisked to Coleraine Causeway Hospital. During my recuperation I had a stent installed in one of my arteries, and slowly but surely got back to work.

Good News Clubs were visited, some school assemblies taught, and, with summer, the Five Day and Holiday Bible Clubs were launched. With camp now in Castlerock it meant that Anne and I could sleep at home. Although we were back at camp we had lots of helpers. With Hugh Moon leading, Roland Brown and I shared the teaching; Anne looked after the bookstall and tuck shop.

During the late summer I had another little upset, but everything checked out all right. However, I found not being able to do everything I wanted to do very frustrating and stressful, so I took a break. During this time a committee member, Rona Taylor, took over the role of area director. A former summer missionary, Jennifer McNeill, who was back home from missionary work in Bolivia, took over the Dungiven, Claudy and Limavady school assemblies. With Anne's agreement I contacted Henry Berry and, once again, handed in our resignations to CEF of Ireland. The organisation held a special evening for Anne and me, to which former workers and our family were invited. Our old friend and mentor, Kenneth Martin, had put together with the help of family a series of slides from past to present, showing many aspects of our lives and ministries both in Ireland and in the Isle of Man. Anne and I were presented with watches engraved with the word 'refocusing'; Henry Berry refused to accept that we were retiring and how right he was! The local committee also organised a special evening for us at a hotel in Campsie, just a few miles outside Londonderry. Again there were special guests and we received lovely tributes. I received lots of 'get well' cards from the schools I had visited. One had a big drawing of Henry, the guitar, on the front. This disturbed Erin, my granddaughter, the younger of Richard and Karen's two girls. She was saddened to think that the children missed Henry more than me.

In Drumahoe, on the outskirts of Londonderry, was the Lismacarol Mission Hall where Anne had once helped in a Good News Club. On our return to north-west Ulster we had held our teacher training there. The leadership had just finished a week of mission at which a number of conversions took place. Joan Lynch, part of the Lismacarol team, phoned me and asked if Anne and I could visit and speak and share on the following Tuesday evening. We were delighted to agree, and thus began a series of weekly Bible teaching evenings which were God-blessed and very fruitful. This continued for the next two years and for me, health-wise, things were great.

During this time our daughter, Karen, and Euan were planning their wedding, so before long as a family we were Scotland bound. The service was held in Perth, and some friends from the Isle of Man were present. Robin Oake, due to Scottish Law, had to become a Church of Scotland minister for a day in order, at Karen's request, to conduct the ceremony.

Richard and his wife Karen, living in Newtownards with their two lovely daughters, Rebekah and Erin aged 12 and 10, announced that they were expecting another baby. Karen, who loved to visit with us in Castlerock, phoned Anne to announce the pregnancy. She then said that with another baby she and Richard would not find travelling to Castlerock easy, so would we think about moving nearer to Newtownards? A lot of thought and prayer went into this, and with Ian and his wife Margaret also living in Newtownards, we wondered if we should indeed move. Another consideration was the close proximity to Belfast, and the docks where the Isle of Man ferry had a berth. After listening to the CEF Conference Bible message from the Reverend Shaw on Abraham's call, I felt convinced but Anne would need to agree. She loved her home in Castlerock, as did I, although I felt we needed to move. In our garage I had a treadmill for walking exercise, especially when the weather was not so good. Anne also used the treadmill and would listen to music while doing so. I persuaded her to listen to Reverend Shaw's message on Abraham, which she did. Still not convinced, Anne suggested that perhaps we could have our bungalow valued. This we did, but the valuation was less than expected. We waited for two months and then tried with a different estate agent. He was more encouraging about the asking price, so we asked him to go ahead and put the bungalow on the market.

Meanwhile we began looking at houses near or in Bangor, but it was after many weeks of searching and praying (and for Anne, heartache) that we found the house to which we believe God led us. We had two clients interested in our Castlerock bungalow, and we listened with amazement as each bid against the other. Eventually one backed out, and we sold to a lady from Holywood, Co Down, for a very acceptable price well above what we had asked. Once again we were on the move, and quickly settled in to our new home in Navar Drive, Bangor. We then transferred our membership from Portstewart to Hamilton Road Baptist, the church Richard, Karen and family attended.

The church in Hamilton Road had a summer outreach to the children and youth of Kircubbin, a village further down the coast. Phil Derrick, one of the elders from Hamilton Road, had moved to Kircubbin with his family, and Karen and Richard were further challenged about moving there in order to plant a new church in the village. Shortly after their baby, whom they named Ethan, was born, Richard, Karen and the family moved to Kircubbin. The Kircubbin Community Church began life in Phil and Sharon's house, and eventually moved to the Community Centre in the village.

One night we received a late call from Richard to tell us that Karen, his wife, had died suddenly. We dressed and headed for Kircubbin to a distressed house. The church elder, Phil, was there along with our church pastor, Adrian Judd. Anne and Richard woke the girls who were surprised to see Granny there. Gently Richard broke the news to Rebekah and Erin, and Anne and he provided comfort. They were sad days, with a packed funeral service in Hamilton Road Baptist Church. The internment was in the local cemetery, with food provided afterwards by the church.

In the years to follow both Karen's mum, Caroline, and Anne provided support, with Caroline coming up weekly from Limavady, and Anne and I travelling down each morning to let Richard off to work and get the girls to school. This continued for two years, during which Caroline and Granddad Sidney took a house near to Kircubbin to help out. Ethan was well cared for, and not just by Caroline and Anne. Jane and Elisa, friends of Karen's, also helped to look after the family, and Madeleine came occasionally from the Isle of Man to give support.

Anne and I also travelled each Sunday to help out in the new Kircubbin Church. I did some preaching and taught a Sunday school class; Anne was part of the team looking after and teaching in the crèche.

Natalie, a young single mum with a son, Jack, joined the church. Jack and Ethan were the same age, and she and Richard had a lot in common. They formed a friendship which blossomed into love and eventually they married when the boys were three years old. The wedding was held in Hamilton Road Baptist Church, conducted by Pastor Judd, and Euan and Karen sang.

During the following months Anne's health deteriorated, and hospital visits followed. The hiatus hernia mentioned earlier had now become progressively worse, and it was decided that a major operation to repair her diaphragm was needed. Major organs were moving into the chest space, so surgery was urgent. The operation took place in the Ulster Hospital with video coverage and students in attendance. Pig tissue was flown in from Scotland, and this was used to extensively repair Anne's diaphragm. Unfortunately, in hospital Anne contracted MRSA which resulted in a breakdown of her wound. I took her home as quickly as I could, and for the next six months Anne was a bed patient with daily attendance by nurses. Madeleine flew over on a few occasions to help out. Eventually Anne made a good recovery, and later tests showed the MRSA to be out of her system.

CHAPTER TEN

Richard and Natalie now had plans for a new start.
Richard writes:

'For Natalie and I, leaving Kircubbin was a long process.
Our first thoughts after getting married were to push on with
our commitment to and passion for the work of the Kircubbin
Community Church. As time went on we introduced initia-
tives to try and move the church deeper into the community,
and make an impact in the area, but our efforts seemed to be
met with little enthusiasm, especially by a few within the
church leadership. Tensions developed and we became less
and less content with the direction and vision of the church.
With hindsight it may well have been a holy discontent given
by God to enable us to make the next step in our journey.

'The decision to leave the Kircubbin church that we
had helped plant was a difficult one but, combined with the
unhappiness of the children and other factors, it became an
inevitable one. So, after a lot of prayer, we took our leave
in August 2011. The house in Kircubbin sold really quickly
and we moved to a rented house in Newtownards, thus beginning a new adventure. The boys changed school, Rebekah

(although she preferred to be known as Becca) started working for ASDA, Erin was already at college in Newtownards and Natalie got a new job in seasonal cattle testing. We identified a new church that appeared to sit beautifully in line with our own vision of God. That church was the Thriving Life Church (TLC) based on the outskirts of Newtownards town. We also put down a deposit on a new build, still in Newtownards, which on completion we moved into.

'The decision to get involved with the Thriving Life Church came about in a God-inspired way when, while looking to choose a church, we believe we were led to attend Vision Sunday at TLC on the first Sunday in September 2011. Gareth, the pastor, set out the church's desire "to see spiritually lost people become passionate, committed followers of Christ". The mission was for a church to be at the heart of the community, meeting the needs of the people both practically and spiritually by finding and influencing the lost right where they were. This struck a deep-seated chord in our lives, and the decision was made to throw in our lot with TLC. Natalie, I and the boys immediately got involved with Serve, a team that ventured out on a Saturday to impact the community in a practical way. After a short time, this became my primary ministry. Natalie signed up to become a volunteer with Christians Against Poverty (CAP), a free debt-counselling ministry with its base centred in TLC for the local area. Jack and Ethan were very excited to find that their Sunday mornings were not spent in main church, but in 'Thriving Kids' with programmes developed exclusively for their age group.

'In answer to our prayers for the family, Erin slowly integrated into the church, making new friends and eventually joining the youth band, 'Luminous', playing in Thriving Kids and occasionally on the main stage. Eventually she was poached as a main singer for the worship team and then, radically, as bass guitarist. She joined a youth small group, and all of this helped to revive her dormant faith in God. She enrolled for a year in Bradford with the Life Church Leadership Academy there, as she sought God for the future.

Becca was invited to join Living Hope Church in the Isle of Man as a church intern, first in Port St Mary and then in the new church plant in Ramsey. She became involved in leading worship, working with youth and kids, administration, and a host of other activities which challenged her and helped build her relationship with God. She continued for another year as an intern with the church in Port St Mary, developing her gifts particularly in worship and youth ministry, and then the following year Becca felt it was time to become a wage-earner so she applied for and was offered a job with the clothing firm Monsoon. She also remained an active volunteer with Living Hope, where she met Joe whom she started dating.

Natalie became the CAP centre manager in 2013 while also getting more and more involved in church life, teaching with Thriving Kids and fundraising for the Building for Life programme at TLC. She became involved with the pastoral needs in the wider church family and contributed to staff meetings and other functions in the church. I was asked to take on the leadership of the community ministry, now renamed Team Serve, and I also joined the Pastoral Care and Christianity Explore teams. We both took on 'small groups' (home Bible studies) as leaders. Natalie's group met in our home in Newtownards while I led a new group in another venue.

'Natalie increased her hours with the church, eventually becoming a full-time church worker, and then she and I were approached by the leaders to join the Senior Leadership Team. We jumped at such an amazing opportunity and are just blessed to be part of a project that's so close to our hearts.'

CHAPTER ELEVEN

Back in the Isle of Man things were happening in the
Port St Mary Church. The church now had a full time
pastor, Jonathan Stanfield. Our son Adrian had accepted a
call to come and take on the role of youth pastor, along with
Madeleine (more about this later). Port St Mary Baptist
Church was growing. Plans to demolish the old crumbling
building and to rebuild a modern structure were put into
action. The church used the local school while the old building
was knocked down and a new church building constructed,
and during this period the church grew in numbers. With the
new church building ready and functioning, and with a new
multimedia and sound system installed, the church decided
that training in using the equipment was needed.

Meanwhile in Scotland Karen was now a physiotherapist in
an Edinburgh clinic. Euan had given up secular employment
and was working with a trust which had a centre in Edinburgh
for Christian music and other events. He was in charge of the
musical and spiritual side of the venture. The trust also had a
studio in Mull, to which Euan would take up-and-coming
Christian musicians and bands for recordings.

The Church in Port St Mary decided to invite Euan and Karen to give training in music and worship. That visit was very successful and then, on another occasion, came a challenge to Euan regarding ministry in the Isle of Man.

Karen takes up the story:

'In 2003 Euan was working for IBM, our eldest, Holly, was nine months old, and I was working part-time as a physiotherapist, when God called Euan into full-time Christian work. Euan had been advising a Christian arts charity (An Airde) about sound systems and recording equipment when they offered him a full-time role, which involved running a music venue in the centre of Edinburgh and a recording studio on the Isle of Mull. It seemed like a mad idea! Euan loved sound engineering and was passionate about music, but this job came with a salary around half of what he was earning at IBM. I remember doing sums on scraps of paper, trying to see if this amount could cover our monthly outgoings and it just didn't add up, yet Euan had a clear picture of standing on a cliff edge with The Lord beside him whispering, "Jump!"

'So we jumped!

'It was a difficult decision as IBM offered a very promising future with financial security, but it is amazing looking back to see how God provided for us over the seven years Euan spent with An Airde. We never went without, and I remember several instances when God came through in miraculous ways. One time we had a bill for £250 which we couldn't pay. I suggested we should do radio jingles to try and earn some more money; Euan laughed at this 'absurd idea', and laughed even harder when the very next morning, out of the blue, someone popped a cheque through our door for the exact amount! I did have the last laugh though, when that afternoon we received a call from a guy from Youth with a Mission who asked, "Do you guys do radio jingles?" So we ended up on

Radio Clyde advertising the upcoming YWAM mission. This was a great time for Euan, working with some amazing Christian and secular musicians, and he also found himself with constant opportunities to share his faith and pray with people. I remember a family friend saying this seemed like good preparation for pastoral work.

'As if!'

'Meanwhile, the church we attended was planting a new congregation to the west of Edinburgh, very near to where we lived, so we were excited to be part of the core team in this new venture. We were involved in various ministries within the life of the church; Euan headed up the sound team and I led the kids' work, but soon worship became our primary focus. Euan and I met through playing in a funk band so we always loved playing and singing together, but we also had a shared passion for leading people into the presence of God through praise and worship.

'My big brother Adrian was youth pastor on the Isle of Man at the time, and he invited us over on a couple of occasions for Euan to train the sound team and worship teams in what was then Port St Mary Baptist Church. Then, in late 2008, we started to feel unsettled, like a stirring of the nest! It was the same feeling that we had before Euan left IBM. I have learned that it can be hard to distinguish the call of God from a bad case of heartburn!

'Then came an even more unsettling conversation with Adrian. On the face of it, there was nothing that should have unsettled us; he was simply telling us about what was happening on the Island, a new church plant into Douglas, a change of name of the church to 'Living Hope Community Church (LHCC)' and the exciting ways in which the Holy Spirit was moving. And we were telling him about the exciting opportunities through the work of An Airde. Sounds ominous?

Not really, but something deep in our spirits was stirring! And it wasn't comfortable!'

'In February 2009, we were again invited to the Isle of Man for a weekend, this time to lead worship, to do a gig in a local café and to meet some of the church leaders. At the time the leadership had started to talk about employing another full-time worker, possibly a pastor for the new congregation in Douglas, or a worship pastor.'

'We had a fantastic weekend, we loved every minute, but why would we even consider leaving Edinburgh? Euan had his family nearby, he was in his 'dream job', we were serving God, my work was going well and the kids (Holly was six and had been joined by a little brother, Conor, who was now three) were settled into school and nursery. Plus, Euan was no pastor; he had never preached in his life. No, it was a nice weekend and it left us even more passionate about leading worship, but that was that!

'Before we left, Euan received a prophetic word from a man who didn't know us or anything about us. He said:

"I see that you have a big decision to make, and God wants you to know the favour of The Lord rests on you."

'The following weekend we were leading worship at our home church, and our good friend Debbie (who didn't know about our trip to the Island or the thoughts going around in our heads) prayed for us. She said that she saw a picture of us leading worship on a big stage with a large band (we had only ever led with acoustic guitar and voices!) and prayed that we would be willing to go wherever God wanted us to go. Then she said:

"God wants you to know that the favour of The Lord rests on you."

'How odd to hear that phrase twice in two weeks!'

'We started listening to the teaching podcasts from Living Hope; they were doing a series on Jonah, the reluctant prophet, and every week the question was asked, "If you are called will you go?" Our home church was doing a series on Abraham, and every week the subject was raised, "If you were called would you go, leave your family and go?"

'When Euan left IBM it was a big sacrifice in terms of prospects and financial security, but God hadn't asked us to leave our beautiful home or family. But to even consider a move from Scotland would mean leaving the place where Euan was born and bred, leaving lifelong friends, leaving his brother Jamie, who is also his best friend, and his parents who were such a huge part of our lives and the lives of our kids!

'When it came time to apply for a role in the church (it was now looking as though the successful applicant would be leading a new church plant as well as overseeing worship across all the congregations), Euan applied even though he didn't want to leave Edinburgh. The application form itself was leaving him all the more convinced that he was in no way qualified or experienced to carry out this role.

"We'll be like Abraham," we thought. "We'll show ourselves willing, while all the time hoping for that ram in the bushes to let us off the hook!"

'We were definitely more like Jonah the reluctant prophet than Abraham the faithful follower!

'Euan was called for interview in June 2009. He was also asked to preach at Port St Mary and Douglas. About three weeks before the interview we started to question whether we were hearing from God at all. Was this all Adrian's crazy idea? Why were we even going along with it? The thought of going was such a painful burden, shouldn't we be feeling peace if this was the right thing? We'd never felt less peaceful in our lives! So we prayed hard! One night we prayed, "Lord, show us an obvious sign that you want us to even go across for the interview". Within minutes of praying, I logged on to

Facebook. I had received a message from a girl called Wendy; I had gone out with her brother when I lived in the Isle of Man and I knew she had also trained as a physiotherapist. I had not seen her for 17 years and then, out of the blue, came this message:

"Hey Karen, are you still in physiotherapy? I don't suppose you're after part-time work in the Isle of Man?"

'I turned to Euan and asked him, "If I was offered a job in the Isle of Man, would that be an obvious sign?"

'Needless to say, we went for the interview. Euan had a 'grilling' from ten leaders and members of the church which lasted three hours, followed by an afternoon with the small group who met in the west of the Island and who would form the core of the new church plant .... more grilling! The next day Euan preached for the first time and was amazing! Not only did he show that God had clearly gifted him to preach, but the message he brought was so timely and relevant and echoed the heartbeat of Living Hope.

'That evening the leaders met to debrief, and I went off to meet Wendy to discuss the physiotherapy job. It so happened that she had been praying for a Christian to come and work in her practice and needed two days covering, which was perfect for me. Euan at last had some 'alone-time'. Still not convinced of a clear calling from God, and feeling saddened and even sick at the thought of leaving his 'home', he prayed and turned to that evening's Bible reading which happened to be the parable of the talents in Luke 19:12-28. The study book he was using followed it up with these three questions:

'Is God calling you to a new ministry?

'Is he calling you to a new place?

'Are you scared to go?

'Tick. Tick. Tick. It concluded using the Message version of verse 26:

"Risk your life and get more than you ever dreamed of. Play it safe and end up holding the bag."

"Okay Lord," he said. "I get the message!"

'When we returned to Scotland we had a week's holiday. "Let's not even talk about the Isle of Man for the next seven days!" we agreed. So Euan took us camping in the most northerly remote part of Scotland; it was an eight-hour drive to get there! When we arrived, we drove to the far end of the campsite and set up our tent, as far away from any other people as possible. A few minutes later a camper van pulled up right next to us, with an Isle of Man registration and slogans all over the van saying 'Isle of Man TT races'. God really has a sense of humour!

'The leaders unanimously offered Euan the job, and the church vote two weeks later was also unanimous. Funnily enough, on the morning of the church vote a man from our home church, who didn't know anything about our journey, shared a verse that he felt God said was for us, those now familiar words, "May the favour of the Lord rest on you" from Psalm 90:17 (NIV).

'So here we are, six years on, serving God in the Isle of Man. Our little congregation in Peel has grown from that little group of 12 adults and eight kids to over 150 people, and God is doing incredible things both in the Isle of Man and across the nations as we partner with churches from all over the world!'

Chapter Twelve

Now, Adrian and Madeleine's story. Adrian writes:
'Following university, I came to join my parents on the Isle of Man where I eventually joined an engineering company. My fiancée Madeleine was nursing in Scotland. After we married, Madeleine and I purchased a home in Ballasalla just around the corner from my parents. Part of my time was spent working with the Stauros group and the Stauros worker, Dewi Lloyd-Humphries, to give him his full name. I felt more drawn to this ministry, and eventually Madeleine (Maddie) and I left our beloved Isle of Man to work full-time with Stauros in their residential home at Ballyards in Co Armagh, Northern Ireland. Towards the end of the third year of residential work we were both feeling quite institutionalised within the strict regime of a unit for people suffering from addictions. We were also probably quite starved of fellowship and spiritual input outside that of the Stauros organisation.

'On a visit to our home church on the Isle of Man our pastor, Jonathan Stanfield, revealed to us that the church was looking to appoint an associate pastor with a particular focus on the youth. I was excited about this and we joked about me applying for that job. I have since learned that many of Jonathan's plans begin with a joke! Maddie and I prayed about this and over the course of a few months we felt that God was leading us back to the Isle of Man, so we applied for the position. In the period leading up to the interview, God confirmed to us, especially through His Word, that we were indeed 'going home'.

'At our home church the interview went well, and I was offered the role of associate pastor. It was time to leave our work with Stauros, sell our home in Ireland and head back to the Isle of Man. It seemed too good to be true. To be returning to the church we love on the Island we adore; surely God doesn't work that way? Is it not supposed to be hardship and sacrifice following God? We soon learned that God's plans are not our plans, but also they can be "immeasurable more than we can imagine or hope for".

'On the Island we moved into a one-bedroom flat in Port St Mary, owned by a family from the church who allowed us to live there rent-free. Then we began the process of building a youth ministry and developing the role of associate pastor working with Jonathan. Maddie started work as a coordinator of a 'live at home' scheme with a charity just starting in the south of the Island.

'Shortly after this we experienced a bitter blow and a great loss to the family. Early one morning I received a call from my brother, Richard, telling Maddie and me that his wife Karen had died suddenly in the night. We just couldn't take it in, but quickly went home to be with Richard and his children. It proved to be a very difficult time as Maddie and I watched Richard and the family have their lives turned upside-down in a moment. One thing Richard said helped me and Maddie to understand our roles in all of the chaos. He simply asked me to be a brother and not a pastor. Maddie travelled to Ireland every few weeks to help support Richard and the children. I believe it was a blessing she was able to do this, and it definitely helped in strengthening the stability of Richard and his family during those painful days.

'Over the next few years we saw both the youth work and the church grow until the building was filled on a Sunday morning. I also saw my own role develop into leading youth teams and training leaders, and in addition taking more of a pastoral and teaching role in the life of the church.

'Our pastor, Jonathan, had been on a sabbatical where he had completed a course involving church planting. On his return the sense of God's leading was that he was positioning the church for growing, and since our building was filled it was obvious that God was leading us to plant a congregation in Douglas. Over half of our numbers were living there and travelling to the south to church every Sunday.

'Before long the decision was taken to plant a congregation, taking about 70 of our Douglas people out of Port St Mary; Jonathan would preach at both services. This worked well initially, but after a year the Douglas congregation had grown to over 120 and needed to have its own pastor. I sensed very strongly that I should offer to take the lead in Port St Mary, and allow Jonathan to focus mainly on the Douglas congregation. The church was very keen on this, and we were sure that this was God's decision as over the next year we built up both congregations. The church also unsuccessfully tried to recruit a pastor to join our team. That was when, as a church, we sensed that God was opening the door to a third congregation, this time in the west of the Island. We had about 20 families attending our church from Peel, so it seemed right to launch a new congregation in Peel supported by resources from both Port St Mary and Douglas for use in worship, children's ministries and preaching. It was clear after a short time that this was the right decision, as the church started to grow and obviously needed its own pastor to continue this growth.

'At around this time I was running an outreach, a group of 20 to 30-year-olds in Douglas called 'Café Church'. Each month I would invite a singer, who was a Christian, to the Island and they would just share their faith through their songs to the 50 or so who joined us in the café. On one occasion I invited my sister Karen, and her husband Euan, over to the Island to sing and share their story. It was then that I felt they had a heart and a calling to lead a church. So the following Christmas, when Maddie and I, Euan, Karen and family, were all in our parents' house in Ireland, I broached the subject about them coming to the Island. I didn't think it went well, maybe I had peaked too soon, but I was sure that I had heard God on this. God was indeed 'on their case', and it wasn't long before Euan and Karen were part of the team and leading the congregation in Peel.

'In the midst of all this crazy church growth and busyness, Maddie and I also came to a significant point in our lives. Ever since nearly day one Maddie and I had planned to have a house full of lively red-headed children, but it had never happened. When we discovered there were medical reasons why we couldn't conceive, we went down the root of medical intervention, but as our doctor eventually told us it was fruitless trying any further. We had gone as far as we could medically, and we had been forward at every healing meeting we attended and received prayer from anyone who wanted to pray for us for a child.

'Amazingly, in God's strength, we have never focused on what we don't have, getting lost in the regrets and loss, although we do miss not having a family. God has blessed us with dozens of spiritual kids who continue to grow into amazing adults, some of whom now have families of their own, and many are serving God in church. God has been faithful and we do have six kids; six Ugandan children we support through 'Compassion', a charity close to our hearts.

'As the ministry in Peel began to flourish and the congregation in Douglas grew, the ministry team began to sense God guiding us to plant another congregation in the north of the Island, in the town of Ramsey. As usual it started with a joke from Jonathan regarding Maddie and I moving north!

'At about that time my friend Rousseau, who had been such a faithful youth leader along with his wife Rhian, was given the opportunity to join the team and lead a congregation. They have a lovely son called Noah who has severe special needs, and as a result their home had been adapted for Noah's needs. That clearly showed Maddie and I that we were the ones to relocate and pioneer a new church plant in Ramsey, with Rousseau taking over the southern congregation.

'Maddie had also just started a new job as the national representative for 'Care for the Family'. Our house didn't sell straightaway so we rented a holiday home in Ramsey, and wonderfully we were joined by our niece Becca; she was going to work with Maddie and I as an intern for a year to help us plant.

'The Ramsey church started with 15 people in our home, and quickly grew to 27 as we moved to twice a month Sunday services at the town hall. God kept adding to our number and new folks got saved, and we eventually moved to a church hall a few miles outside Ramsey. Facility-wise it was not the best of locations, but there the congregation again began to grow. We have since moved into a new venue, the local high school, a real answer to prayer, as we continue to impact our Ramsey and district community for Jesus. So far no new jokes from Jonathan, so we are settled.'

Chapter Thirteen

The Roy and Anne story continues:

During the early days in Bangor at Hamilton Road Baptist Church, I helped in the Sunday school and with preaching. Anne and I also shared our story in various meetings. I preached several Sundays in another local Baptist church, and conducted Sunday school services and midweek meetings in this and other churches. Unfortunately, my health again caused problems and I ended up making several visits to hospital for check-ups, especially with regard to heart failure. Another stent was inserted but my preaching and teaching ministry became very much on hold, yet Anne and I are busy writing to, phoning and praying for various missionary organisations with which we are in touch.

Another setback to our mobility occurred in June 2013 when Anne missed her footing on the stairs one night at bedtime. She fell badly and ended up in hospital where X-rays showed two broken ankle bones and a shattered fibula. Anne was in hospital on two occasions for operations, and had several visits to the fracture clinic. She now has pins in her ankles and a metal plate on the fibula.

My heart continued to present me with problems resulting in several hospital stays, during which much was promised but little done except to experiment with medicine changes. I had a blackout in church on a Sunday morning in July 2014, which brought about another stay in hospital. This time I was sent home with a seven-day heart monitor which showed up a number of significant problems. I had four more blackouts and hospital visits, during which again nothing was done except for more medicine changes. I decided to make a private appointment with a cardiologist at a Belfast clinic. I had made out a history of my heart upsets from my heart attack to the present day and, when the cardiologist read this, he admitted me within a week to the Royal Victoria Hospital in Belfast. Tests there showed several instances of heart fibrillation which resulted in the installation of an ICD (Implantable Cardioverter Defibrillator). This has led to a significant improvement in my heart rhythms and, although I am still a heart failure patient and attend the clinic in the local hospital, life is much more enjoyable.

Regarding the future; we are slowly coming to terms with our health problems and limited mobility. We continue to enjoy our times of prayer for, and contact with, the missionary and church organisations that we support. Everything else is committed into God's hands.

(The titles Good News Clubs, Five Day Clubs, Holiday Bible Clubs, Senior and Junior Youth Challenge are copyright and registered to the Child Evangelism Fellowship.)

(Stauros® - The **Stauros** Foundation is an evangelistic agency that helps people who have addiction issues and offers support to their families)